ULTIMATE GUIDE

CERAMIC & STONE
TILING

ULTIMATE GUIDE

CERAMIC & STONE
TILING

CREATIVE HOMEOWNER®

ULTIMATE GUIDE: CERAMIC & STONE TILING

MANAGING EDITOR	Fran J. Donegan
CONTRIBUTING EDITORS	Steve Willson, Mike McClintock
PROOFREADER	Sara M. Markowitz
PHOTO COORDINATOR, DIGITAL IMAGING	Mary Dolan
INDEXER	Schroeder Indexing Services
LAYOUT	David Geer, Glee Barre
PRINCIPAL PHOTOGRAPHER	John Parsekian
PHOTO ASSISTANTS	Dan Lane, Dan Houghtaling
	James Parlagi
ILLUSTRATIONS	Robert LaPointe
ART DEVELOPMENT	Glee Barre

Current Printing (last digit)
10 9 8 7 6 5

Manufactured in China

Ultimate Guide: Ceramic & Stone Tiling, Third Edition
Previously published as *Ultimate Guide to Ceramic & Stone Tile*
Library of Congress Control Number: 2011932130
ISBN-10: 1-58011-546-2
ISBN-13: 978-1-58011-546-9

CREATIVE HOMEOWNER®
www.creativehomeowner.com

Creative Homeowner books are distributed by
Fox Chapel Publishing
1970 Broad Street
East Petersburg, PA 17520
www.FoxChapelPublishing.com

Safety

Although the methods in this book have been reviewed for safety, it is not possible to overstate the importance of using the safest methods you can. What follows are reminders—some do's and don'ts of work safety—to use along with your common sense.

- Always use caution, care, and good judgment when following the procedures described in this book.
- Always be sure that the electrical setup is safe, that no circuit is overloaded, and that all power tools and outlets are properly grounded. Do not use power tools in wet locations.
- Always read container labels on paints, solvents, and other products; provide ventilation; and observe all other warnings.
- Always read the manufacturer's instructions for using a tool, especially the warnings.
- Use hold-downs and push sticks whenever possible when working on a table saw. Avoid working short pieces if you can.
- Always remove the key from any drill chuck (portable or press) before starting the drill.
- Always pay deliberate attention to how a tool works so that you can avoid being injured.
- Always know the limitations of your tools. Do not try to force them to do what they were not designed to do.
- Always make sure that any adjustment is locked before proceeding. For example, always check the rip fence on a table saw or the bevel adjustment on a portable saw before starting to work.
- Always clamp small pieces to a bench or other work surface when using a power tool.
- Always wear the appropriate rubber gloves or work gloves when handling chemicals, moving or stacking lumber, working with concrete, or doing heavy construction.
- Always wear a disposable face mask when you create dust by sawing or sanding. Use a special filtering respirator when working with toxic substances and solvents.
- Always wear eye protection, especially when using power tools or striking metal on metal or concrete; a chip can fly off, for example, when chiseling concrete.
- Never work while wearing loose clothing, open cuffs, or jewelry; tie back long hair.

- Always be aware that there is seldom enough time for your body's reflexes to save you from injury from a power tool in a dangerous situation; everything happens too fast. Be alert!
- Always keep your hands away from the business ends of blades, cutters, and bits.
- Always hold a circular saw firmly, usually with both hands.
- Always use a drill with an auxiliary handle to control the torque when using large-size bits.
- Always check your local building codes when planning new construction. The codes are intended to protect public safety and should be observed to the letter.
- Never work with power tools when you are tired or when under the influence of alcohol or drugs.
- Never cut tiny pieces of wood or pipe using a power saw. When you need a small piece, saw it from a securely clamped longer piece.
- Never change a saw blade or a drill or router bit unless the power cord is unplugged. Do not depend on the switch being off. You might accidentally hit it.
- Never work in insufficient lighting.
- Never work with dull tools. Have them sharpened, or learn how to sharpen them yourself.
- Never use a power tool on a workpiece—large or small—that is not firmly supported.
- Never saw a workpiece that spans a large distance between horses without close support on each side of the cut; the piece can bend, closing on and jamming the blade, causing saw kickback.
- When sawing, never support a workpiece from underneath with your leg or other part of your body.
- Never carry sharp or pointed tools, such as utility knives, awls, or chisels, in your pocket. If you want to carry any of these tools, use a special-purpose tool belt that has leather pockets and holders.

Contents

CERAMIC AND STONE TILE are truly unique building materials. Tile is available in an almost endless variety of shapes and colors to suit any house style and any taste. And tile offers a combination of qualities you won't find in many other building materials—it's extremely durable; you can install it indoors or outdoors, in wet or dry locations; it doesn't rot or burn or provide a nesting space or food source for insects. If you install it correctly, tile is one of the few materials that should last as long as your house without a major update or a complete replacement.

introduction

Because of its resistance to water, tile is often used in bathrooms, right. Note the decorative tile backsplash and the tile border around the mirror.

A change in tile design defines the different areas of this kitchen, opposite.

Granted, it takes a little longer to install tile than it does to lay down a carpet or slap up a sheet of drywall. But in this book you'll find complete details and step-by-step photos to take you through every type of tile job. You'll get sensible, understandable help with selecting the right materials, using tools safely and effectively, and preparing both existing and new areas for tile jobs that last.

You'll be able to tile kitchens and counters, baths and vanities, floors and walls—using the same techniques as the professionals. And just in case someone drops a heavy pot on your new floor, there's also a complete section on repairs and maintenance.

GUIDE TO SKILL LEVEL

 Easy. Made for beginners.

 Challenging. Can be done by beginners who have the patience and willingness to learn.

 Difficult. Can be handled by most experienced do-it-yourselfers who have mastered basic construction skills. Consider consulting a specialist.

tile basics

1

MODERN CERAMIC AND STONE TILES provide hundreds of design options that can enhance floors, walls, countertops, and other areas of the home. From a practical standpoint, tile is easier to install than it has been in the past. The old-fashioned method of installation, called "thick-set," which required a solid mortar bed to serve as the base for the tile, isn't used on most applications. In today's "thinset" applications, you simply embed the tiles in tile adhesive over plywood, drywall, cement backer board, or some other approved substrate. With proper preparation, a ceramic or stone tile installation should provide years of service.

A SHORT HISTORY OF TILE

The earliest forms of ceramic tile date back to prehistoric times, when the use of clay as a building material was developed independently in several early cultures. The precursors of modern tile were roughly shaped and not nearly as strong as tiles today. The material was dug from river banks, roughly formed into building blocks, and baked dry in the sun. The first tiles were crude, but even 6,000 years ago people were decorating them by adding pigments for color and carving low-relief designs into their surfaces.

Firing Tile

The ancient Egyptians were the first to discover that firing clay tiles at high temperatures in a kiln made them stronger and more water-resistant. Many ancient cultures also used thin squares of fired clay as decorative elements in their architecture.

Buildings in ancient Mesopotamian cities were fronted with unglazed terra-cotta and colorful decorative tiles. Ancient Greeks and Romans used ceramics for the floors, roofs, and even the plumbing in their buildings. The Chinese used a white clay called *kaolin* to develop the white-colored and durable ceramic known as porcelain.

Tiles in medieval Europe were generally reserved for the floors of churches. Across the continent, the Byzantines excelled in using tile at a small scale; they created expressive mosaic patterns and murals using ceramic tile as well as pieces of glass and stone.

Glazing Tile

Persian ceramicists, inspired by imported Chinese porcelain, created a decorative tradition that spread across South Asia, North Africa, into Spain with the Moors, and eventually throughout Europe. Because their Islamic religion prohibited using human images in art, artisans turned to brightly colored tiles with ornate and intertwined patterns.

Solid-color glazed tiles were cut and assembled into large-scale mosaics with subtle color gradations. The Islamic artisans also developed metal-oxide glazes using tin, copper, cobalt, manganese, and antimony, which made tile glazes more brilliant and durable.

By the fifteenth century, metal-oxide-glazed tile had become popular in Italy, and their design influence moved northward with Italian craftsmen. Major European trading centers gave their names to local design motifs and types of tile that are still used, including delft tile (from Delft in Holland), and majolica tile (from Majorca in Spain).

Modern Tile

Today, most commercial tile manufacturers use the pressed-dust method of construction. First, a mixture of ingredients is pressed into the desired tile shape. Then the tile is glazed (or left unglazed) and baked in a kiln. Some tile makers may extrude tile shapes by squeezing them through a press into a die or by rolling them out flat and cutting the tile shapes with a form much like a cookie cutter.

Whatever the method, all ceramic tile must be fired to become durable. The purity of the clay, the number of firings, and the temperature of the kiln determine the quality and price. Kiln temperatures vary from just below 2,000°F to 2,500°F. Lower firing temperatures produce more porous tile and soft glazes; higher temperatures produce dense, nonporous tile and hard glazes.

Decorative tiles were used in complex color and pattern combinations, as on this ancient building in Jerusalem.

Modern mosaics and combinations of stock and hand-made tiles can be just as intricate as ancient patterns.

Ancient artisans created intricate shapes with small tiles, such as this pattern in a church at Mount Nebo in Jordan.

TILE CHARACTERISTICS

There are several types of ceramic tile and many ways to categorize them. The built-in properties can make one better than another for a particular installation.

Firing and Glazes

When most tile is first formed, it has to dry enough to become stable. Then it goes into a kiln at temperatures ranging from about 1,800°F to 2,500°F. Tiles fired at lower temperatures generally are more porous and have softer glazes than tiles fired at higher temperatures.

These surface coatings can be used to add color and decoration, and to protect the tile body. Color is commonly included in a mixture of pigments that is added before the tile is fired or applied to a hardened tile and bonded with a second firing. Glazed tiles range from a high-gloss to a dull matte finish.

Water Absorption

There are four basic categories of tile rated by how much water they absorb. More-porous tiles are generally softer and absorb more water. Less-porous tiles generally are harder and may be more expensive than more porous tiles.

Nonvitreous tile absorbs about 7 percent or more water; semivitreous tile absorbs between 3 percent and 7 percent water; vitreous tile absorbs between 0.6 percent and 3 percent water; and impervious tile absorbs 0.5 percent or less water. Generally, the longer the firing time and the higher the firing temperature, the more nonporous (or vitreous) the tile. Vitreous and impervious tiles include ceramic and glass mosaic varieties, as well as porcelain tiles. Don't use nonvitreous or semivitreous tiles outdoors in cold climates. Water trapped in the tile body will alternately freeze and thaw, cracking the tile.

Tile porosity becomes important in the choice of tiles for wet conditions such as a tub surround because water absorbed by porous tiles can harbor bacteria and eventually penetrate the substrate, loosening the tile bond.

Tile Selection

When you visit your tile dealer, the ceramic tile probably will be divided into basic categories of wall, floor, and ceramic mosaic tile. There are also many specialty tiles. (See pages 18 to 33 for more on tile materials.)

Tile can connect one area of the home to another, such as shown in this bathroom and adjoining laundry room.

Ceramic tiles with interlocking patterns can form a centerpiece by themselves or in a surrounding field of tile.

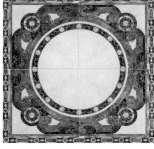

While ancient mosaics were installed piece by piece (left), intricate patterns are now available on full tiles (right).

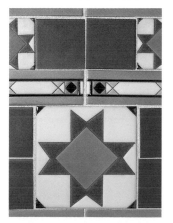

Larger tiles, trim strips, and accent tiles can be combined into highly decorative and colorful panels.

Floor Tiles. Most glazed floor tiles work on countertops and other horizontal surfaces subject to heavy use. Some may be too heavy to set on walls without special supports during the installation, such as a batten board or a row of nails. Some come in sizes up to 24 inches square and may be unwieldy and out of scale as wall tile. Glazed floor tiles often are listed in manufacturers' catalogs as glazed quarry tile or glazed pavers. Generally, you use glazed floor tiles on interior floors only. But some glazed floor tiles have a fine carbide grit incorporated into the glaze to make them slip-resistant in wet areas.

Wall Tiles. Wall tiles generally are thin, lightweight, nonvitreous (porous) tiles coated with a soft glaze. Most don't have the strength to stand up to floor traffic. You also can use sheet tile mounted on a backing of paper, plastic mesh, or fabric mesh. The sheets eliminate the laborious process of spacing individual tiles.

Ceramic Mosaic Tiles. All tiles that are 2 inches square or smaller are considered mosaic tiles. Generally, these dense-bodied vitreous tiles resist water, stains, impact, frost, and abrasion, making them suitable for practically any application. Shapes include squares, rectangles, hexagons, circles, teardrops, clover leafs, and random pebble designs, among others. Most ceramic mosaic tiles are mounted on a backing sheet.

Antique Tiles. Although some rare old tiles command very high prices, others are relatively affordable. All are collectible, including Victorian art tiles, Arts-and-Crafts tiles, and Art-Deco tiles, among others. If you can't find the real thing, check with companies specializing in imported hand-painted tiles. Many include a selection of reproduction antique designs.

Hand-Painted and Mural Tiles. Large tile manufacturers offer a broad selection of domestic and imported hand-painted tiles. Several even employ a staff of artists to make personalized hand-painted tiles to order, as do small independent artisans and ceramic shops. Hand-painted tiles are available as individual accents to spruce up a kitchen countertop or fireplace surround. Some hand-painted tiles have sculptured surfaces, while others are hand-cut into unusual shapes. Custom-made hand-painted tiles vary widely in price—from $20 to $100 per piece—depending on whether they are chosen from stock designs or are custom-made to your specifications. If hand-painted tiles are too costly, most tile dealers also carry decorator tiles and picture tiles with silk screen or decal designs at a more affordable price.

Tile Basics

TILE SIZES AND SHAPES

Field tiles come in several different shapes, which you can use singly or in various combinations to form patterns. The actual size of these tiles may vary 1/8 inch more or less, as will the thickness, depending on the manufacturer. This means you can't always mix tiles from different manufacturers, so it is important to make sure that you buy enough tiles from a single source before you start the project.

Single Tiles

This is the type of ceramic tile that most do-it-yourselfers use: single tiles laid one at a time. They are available in a great variety of sizes, colors, and patterns. Most custom decorative and hand-painted tiles fall into this category as well. Tiles typically are 1/4 to 3/8 inch thick and range in size from 1 x 1 inch to 12 x 12 inches square, although larger sizes and different shapes are available. Most often, a tile layout will consist of a grid of full-size field tiles that cover most of the area and at least some partial tiles around the edges. The size you find listed in a manufacturer's catalog generally is nominal and not actual. It generally includes an allowance for grout.

Sheet-Mounted Tiles

Sheet tiles are evenly spaced tiles mounted on a backing sheet of paper, plastic mesh, or fabric mesh. They may also may be joined by small dabs of vinyl, polyurethane, or silicone rubber in a process called dot-mounting. Many sheets are 12 inches square or larger. It's wise to use sheet-mounted applications, if available, when installing small tiles that would be very time-consuming to set one by one. All sheet-mounted tiles require grouting once installed.

Pregrouted Tile Panels

Eliminating the need to grout joints sounds like a good idea. And some tile outlets may offer pregrouted tile panels to do the job. But the grout is actually a flexible polyure-thane, polyvinyl chloride, rubber grout, or silicone caulk. Without rigid grout between tiles, these sheets often are flexible enough to bend and stretch with normal building movement. You use tubes of matching silicone caulk to grout the joints between panel edges and trim pieces. Typically, the grout is treated with a special mildew and fungus inhibitor, making these panels suitable for shower and tub enclosures. Because of this chemical treatment, the Food and Drug Administration does not recommend installing the sheets on kitchen countertops or on other serving and food-preparation areas.

BASIC SIZES AND SHAPES

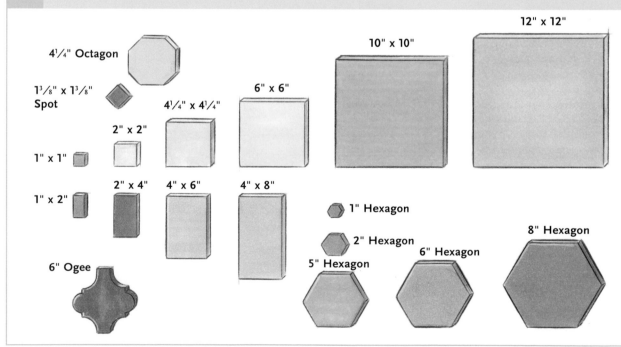

4 1/4" Octagon

1 3/8" x 1 3/8" Spot

4 1/4" x 4 1/4"

2" x 2"

6" x 6"

10" x 10"

12" x 12"

1" x 1"

2" x 4"

4" x 6"

4" x 8"

1" x 2"

1" Hexagon

2" Hexagon

6" Ogee

5" Hexagon

6" Hexagon

8" Hexagon

TRIM AND SPECIALTY TILE

ALL TILES that are not field tiles are referred to as trim tiles. They are used to create finished edges.

Angles. These tiles include inside and outside corners that create sharp turns instead of rounded edges.

Aprons. Half-size tiles called aprons are used to fill in narrow areas, such as along the front of a countertop.

Bases. Tiles designed specifically for the floor line, called base trims or runners, have a finished top edge. They are used where the floor has been tiled but the wall has not.

Beads. These trims are sometimes called quarter-rounds and are used to finish off corners and edges. The narrow pieces turn a rounded, 90-degree angle.

Bullnose. These are field tiles with one curved and finished edge. They neatly trim a course of tile that ends without turning a corner. Often, a bullnose tile is paired with an apron tile meeting the bullnose at a right angle. The result is a smoothly turned edge. There are separate bullnose tiles designed for thin-set and mortar-bed installations.

Countertop Trims. These trim pieces are set on the outside edge of a countertop. The raised lip is designed to prevent drips. Many V-cap tiles have this feature.

Coves. These pieces are used to gently turn corners at a right angle. The corner can turn either inward or outward. Cove base turns a corner at floor level. Special cove pieces that have a finished edge turn a corner at the top row of a backsplash. Other cove pieces do not have finished edges.

Miters. Two miter pieces together form a corner separated by a grout joint.

Rounds. These trim tiles create a rounded corner instead of an angular one.

Swimming-Pool Edging. These tiles are designed to cover the coping on swimming pools. They require a thick-set mortar bed.

V-caps. Although they are called V-shaped, these edging tiles often are more L-shaped to cover the perimeter of a counter, for example, and wrap around the front edge of plywood and backer board.

Windowsill Trim. Windowsill tile has a finished edge on one side and a rounded corner on the other. It covers the sill itself and turns to meet the tile on the wall. Without this trim piece, you would need two tiles: a flat field tile for the sill itself and a quarter-round to turn the corner.

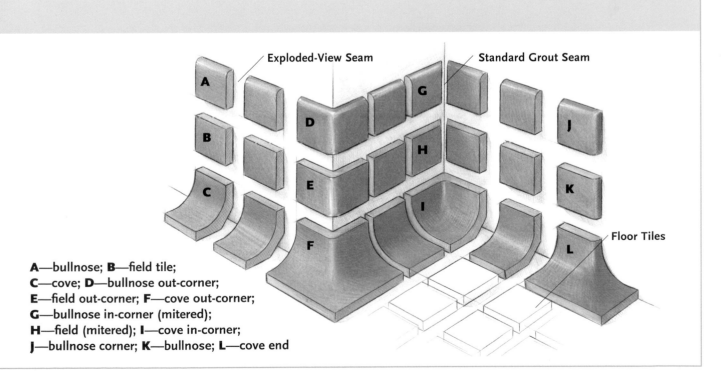

Exploded-View Seam   Standard Grout Seam

Floor Tiles

A—bullnose; B—field tile;
C—cove; D—bullnose out-corner;
E—field out-corner; F—cove out-corner;
G—bullnose in-corner (mitered);
H—field (mitered); I—cove in-corner;
J—bullnose corner; K—bullnose; L—cove end

Tile Basics

CERAMIC TILE

CERAMIC TILE isn't very complicated. Most pieces are nothing more than some clay flattened into a square shape, covered with a hard glaze, and baked in a very high temperature oven. Pretty simple. It's also been around for a while—from what we can tell, about 6,000 years. As such, it's a clear-cut example of established technology. Not much need for a computer chip in these things, at least not right now.

The term might be as clear as a prophet and as old as the hills, but unfortunately, it's a little general. So many different tiles, used in so many different places, are all called ceramic, so buying tile can be a bit confusing. Probably the best way out of the fog is to think of ceramic tile as the default product among many other specialized offerings. It's the stuff on your bathroom walls, your brother-in-law's vanity top, and around the top edge of your neighbor's swimming pool.

Ceramic tile comes in a variety of different sizes, colors, and surface finishes. These days, it's usually installed over a cementitious backer board and embedded in a layer of thinset mortar. Tile is rated by its water resistance. A rating by PEI (Porcelain Enamel Institute) of 1 or 2 means that the tile can be used only on walls. A rating of 3 or 4 makes a tile suitable for all residential applications: floors, walls, and countertops.

The difference between the ratings is primarily the result of how the tile is made. A low temperature (under 2,000°F) firing in the kiln will create a more porous tile, which would be bad for a floor where exposure to moisture is high. When a tile is fired at a higher temperature (about 2,500°F or more) the result is a denser tile with a harder surface that can be used in any residential application anywhere.

Walls and Borders

Ceramic Shower Surround

Two-Toned Color Scheme

Ceramic Accents

Patterned Backsplash

PORCELAIN TILE

ALTHOUGH PORCELAIN TILE can sometimes look like common ceramic tile, there are some big differences. First off, porcelain units are made of carefully refined white clay that is fired at an extremely high temperature. As a result, the individual tiles are very dense and much less porous than ceramic tile, which makes them more water resistant. Porcelain tile is also much harder than ceramic tile, so it wears better and longer and is almost impossible to stain. This makes porcelain a good choice for floors and countertops inside the house and for exterior applications where the freeze-and-thaw cycle is an issue.

Another difference: most porcelain tiles are not glazed. The color of the tile is achieved by colored dyes that are added to the clay during manufacturing. Because of this, the same color goes throughout the entire tile, instead of being only in the glaze. So if the floor is scratched, the damage is less noticeable. The lack of glaze also allows for some subtlety in surface texture. Finer, more intricate patterns can be pressed into the tile. If glaze were added to these tiles, this texture would be lost. The lack of glaze also allows porcelain tile to look more like natural stone tile. With the addition of appropriate color and surface details, porcelain can mimic granite, marble, slate, and other stone products.

In most cases, porcelain tiles are installed like ceramic tiles. This means over a cementitious backer board and in thinset mortar. The mortar should, however, be latex reinforced. Because the porcelain tiles are so dense, they don't absorb much mortar, so the stronger bond achieved by latex additives is required.

Porcelain Floor Tiles

Geometric Pattern

Stone Look-Alike

Stone Backsplash

Terra-Cotta Backsplash

Tile Basics

STONE TILE

MANY TYPES OF NATURAL STONE TILES are available for residential use, both for the inside and outside of the house. The most popular are probably granite, marble, and slate. Of the three, granite is the hardest and densest. It usually comes with a polished surface that makes it water- and stain-resistant. Marble is softer than granite and slate is softer than marble. Both need to be sealed to prevent staining and water damage.

Stone tile tends to cost more per square foot (often $5 to $10) compared to ceramic tile (in the neighborhood of $2 to $3 per foot). But stone tiles have such a distinctive appearance that many people find them irresistible. The variable colors and patterns that are found in natural stone can't be reproduced anywhere else, and no two tiles are exactly alike.

For interior use, granite and marble are usually sold with both surfaces cut smooth and at a consistent thickness. Slate is often sold with one side split and the other side (that will face down into the mortar) cut flat. This yields a somewhat rough floor surface with good traction that many people prefer for kitchens, foyers, and mudrooms. The most popular size is 12 x 12 inches. But many others sizes are available for creating patterns.

Stone tiles require an underlayment of cementitious backer board and are usually set in latex reinforced thinset mortar. Most people seem to prefer very thin grout joints for granite and marble, and a wider grout joint (up to about $3/8$ in.) for slate. One of the drawbacks of using stone tiles is the limited selection of trim pieces. This isn't usually a problem on floors, but it can be more frustrating on walls and countertops.

Marble Tub Surround

Slate Entry

Tumbled Marble Walls

Stone Insets

Granite Walls

GLASS TILE

GLASS TILES, as the name indicates, are made of pieces of glass formed into standard tile sizes. Countless colors and many different textures are available, from smooth to rough. At the extremes, these tiles can be almost transparent and nearly opaque. For the most part, glass tiles are used as accent tiles, almost always on walls. Perhaps the most popular location is on a kitchen countertop backsplash. Glass may be impervious to stains and water damage, but it is prone to cracking and scratching.

Glass tiles have a completely different appearance than typical ceramic tiles because light moves through all but the most opaque pieces. This makes the tiles seem to vibrate slightly, which catches the eye. Add to this the fact that many of the available color options are very vibrant, and you get something that doesn't fade into the background. Glass tiles look more like stained glass, Tiffany lamps, and fruit-flavored hard candy than they do the standard white ceramic tile.

This product is pretty expensive. Prices of $15 per square foot are not uncommon. When you compare glass with ceramic tile that costs $2 to $3 a square foot, it's easy to see why glass tiles are often used as accents. These tiles are also commonly available in mosaic sheets of 1-inch tiles.

As with most other tiles, glass units should be installed over cementitious backer board. But instead of standard thinset mortar, choose a white latex reinforced thinset mortar. Because you can see through most glass tiles, the white background changes the color of the tile less than a dark-gray mortar would. Standard grout is recommended for glass tile. But because the glass is so impervious to any moisture, it takes longer to set than it would with ceramic tile.

Bright-Red Accents

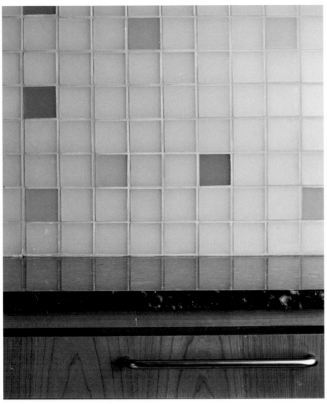

Transparent Design

Shimmering Wall Treatment

Sparkling Backsplash

Tile Basics

TERRA-COTTA TILE

TERRA-COTTA, which means "cooked earth" in Italian, is one of the oldest and most popular tiles in the world. And in many places, it has been made the same way for centuries. Unlike typical ceramic tiles, traditional terra-cotta tiles are not glazed. They are made of unrefined clay baked at comparatively low temperature. Their color is dependent on where the clay comes from. Large producers of terra-cotta like Italy, Portugal, and Mexico have different colors. But tiles from the same country and the same batch can still have a good deal of variation in their hue. This lack of uniformity is considered an attribute, not a failing, to terra-cotta buyers.

Because most terra-cotta tiles lack glaze and are very porous, they soak up water easily. So they need to be sealed thoroughly after they're installed, and resealed periodically to keep them looking their best. Otherwise, staining is inevitable. This natural porosity also prevents terra-cotta from being installed outside if it will be exposed to freezing temperatures.

Terra-cotta tiles come in a wide range of shapes and sizes. Some are nearly as uniform in dimension as ceramic tile. But many terra-cotta products are hand made and therefore vary in size and thickness quite a bit. For interior applications, terra-cotta should be applied over a cementitious backer board and in a bed of latex reinforced thinset mortar. In recent years, glazed terra-cotta tiles have become much more popular. A wide range of brilliant color alternatives is available, as are tiles with hand-painted drawings and engravings.

Traditional Coloring

Contemporary Coloring

Diagonal Pattern

Rustic Elegance

Cooking Center Application

DECORATIVE TILE BORDERS

ALTHOUGH CERAMIC TILE is a wonderful surface finish that is considered by most people to be an upscale design choice, a whole wall or floor of one kind of tile can seem a little monolithic, a little bit like too much of a good thing. This is where decorative borders come to the rescue. These borders can be as simple as a contrasting color of the same tile installed around the perimeter of a kitchen floor. Or they can be more elaborate, like an entirely different type, size, shape, and color of tile used as a kind of chair rail on a bathroom wall.

Border tiles are often high gloss, brightly colored, and heavily textured. Tile stores may have lots of different choices when it comes to field tiles (the ones you use for most of a floor or wall) but will have many fewer decorative tiles. Decorative units can be expensive and a whole wall or floor of these tiles can be visually overwhelming.

Fortunately, the Internet is loaded with different tile design studios that may have decorative tiles that you like. One of the most distinctive types of wall borders is called listello tile. These tiles are usually thicker than the field tiles, so they will stand proud of the wall. They also have molded or embossed patterns, and the most expensive versions are hand painted.

If you plan to integrate a decorative border into a field of standard ceramic tiles, make sure the sizes of the tiles are compatible. Take one of your field tiles along when shopping for decorative units. No matter what you choose, the installation requirements for the decorative tiles will be the same as for the field tiles you are putting on the wall or floor.

Border Styles

Seashell Theme

Playful Accents

Adding Texture

Bright Frames

Tile Basics

PAINTED TILE

PAINTED TILE is really a subset of all tiles. If you want to go through the trouble, any tile can be painted and then glazed or sealed. The only real question is how expensive it will be. It's not unheard of for an individual 4 x 4-inch painted tile to cost nearly $100. But a much more common price is between $10 and $30. That's a lot of money, but if used judiciously, painted tiles can have a tremendous impact on a room without breaking the budget.

One of the most effective uses of these tiles is in a wall mural. These are often designed for the backsplash area above the kitchen countertop or the inside of a tiled shower stall. For centuries, mosaic tiles have been painted to create striking landscapes, portraits, and still lifes that were incorporated into the overall design of floors, walls, and even ceilings.

Some painted tiles are called art tiles. This term generally refers to hand-made units that are used as accents in other tile installations. As you might expect, these tiles are available in a wide range of colors, sizes, and designs—in fact, there are as many types as there are artisans creating them. Depending on how these tiles are made, they may not be as durable as typical manufactured tiles. Make sure the ones you select will perform well where you plan to use them. If this can't be determined, use these tiles only in areas that don't get much wear or exposure to moisture.

You can create painted accent tiles yourself if you are lucky enough to have a ceramic craft store nearby. Some of these places will let you paint blank tiles, and then they'll coat them with a clear glaze and fire them so that they will perform like a manufactured tile.

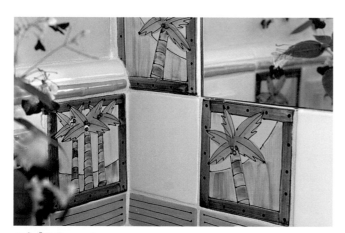

Bright Accents

Fireplace Accents

Cooking Center Theme

Mood Setters

MOSAIC TILE

ONE WAY TO GAUGE PROGRESS over the years is to look at mosaic tile. For centuries, these small tiles (usually ¾- to 2-inch squares) were set individually no matter what the size of the job. A cathedral was treated pretty much the same way as the entry area to a typical home. But finally someone came up with the idea of joining these tiles together in 12-inch-square mats with the tiles glued to a mesh. If you were using 1-inch tiles on a job, laying down one of these sheets made things go about 144 times faster. Not bad, no matter how you define progress.

Today mosaic tiles come in different sizes, shapes, colors, and materials—though glazed ceramic tile and porcelain tile are the most popular. They are commonly used on floors and walls and are installed over cementitious backer board in a bed of thinset mortar.

The small size, however, makes them very popular for other striking treatments, including decorative borders, murals, and one-of-a-kind custom renderings for the luxury residential market. You can also get individual mosaic tiles, instead of sheets, if you just want to accent a plain field of single-color tile or create your own custom border design.

The small size of mosaic tile is not only distinctive, it also makes for easier installation, especially around pipes and other obstructions. All you have to do to remove a tile is cut it from the mesh backing with a utility knife. In fact, mosaic tiles are the product of choice if you're tiling curved or rounded surfaces. Another plus for mosaic floor tiles is the great traction they yield because they have so many grout joints per square foot of floor space.

Custom Application

Traditional Design

Mosaic Border

Colorful Design

Themed Backsplash

Tile Basics

ROOM PREP: STRUCTURE

STRIPPING DRYWALL

By using partial tiles and adjusting the layout of field tiles, you can compensate for minor irregularities on walls. But sometimes you need to do more to prepare an old surface. When you need to strip away drywall, take a cautious approach to avoid cutting or damaging pipes and wires that could be in the wall. If there are outlets, radiators, or hot-air registers close by, you should peel the surface instead of trying more vigorous demolition.

Finding Seams. If the drywall is so well-taped that you can't spot the seams, use a stud finder to locate the vertical strip of nails over studs. The stud with two rows is under the seam between panels.

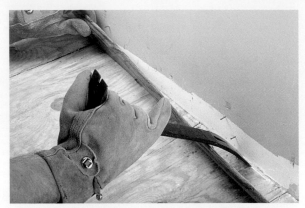

1 The first step is to pull any trim on top of the panel you need to remove. Pry baseboards and other pieces with a flat bar placed over studs.

REMOVING A STUD WALL

When you find one or two studs that are throwing the wall out of kilter or studs damaged by rot, replace them. Because wall studs are nailed through horizontal pieces at the top and bottom of the wall, you can't get at these nails to pull them. The most practical plan is to cut the stud you want to remove in half and pry out the pieces one at a time. If you are replacing several studs in a load-bearing wall, the safest approach is to install one or two temporary braces until the new studs are in place.

Trimming Nails. Where sharp nails remain in the top and bottom frame of the wall, slice them off flush with a reciprocating saw fitted with a metal-cutting blade.

1 Use a reciprocating saw or a saber saw to start cutting through the damaged stud about halfway up the wall. Stay clear of pipes or wires.

ADDING STUDS AND BLOCKING

To beef up a weak stud, or double up framing to provide additional support for new drywall, you can add a stud with construction adhesive and screws. This generally makes a more secure connection than nails alone, and it is less likely to disrupt the finish on nearby wall surfaces. If you have the wall frame exposed, it's also wise to install blocking, such as 2x4s on the flat, wherever you will attach fittings through tile, such as towel racks or grab bars.

Recording Blocking Locations. Before covering wall blocking with new drywall, measure and record its exact distance from the floor. This beats drilling holes through your new tile that turn out to be in the wrong places.

1 Plan the location of grab bars, towel racks, and other similar fittings ahead of time, and mark the height of the fittings on wall studs.

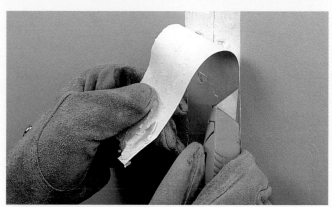

2 Once you locate the seam, use a utility knife to cut through the coats of compound. Peel away the paper tape to expose nailed edges of the panels.

3 After you pull some of the nails, pry on the panel, which will crack in large sections. Then pull the remaining nails in the studs.

2 To keep the stud from binding on the saw blade (even if you cut by hand) insert a wedge to keep the cut open as you complete the job.

3 Once you cut through, pry out the stud in two pieces. Remember to trim the nails driven through the top and bottom of the wall frame.

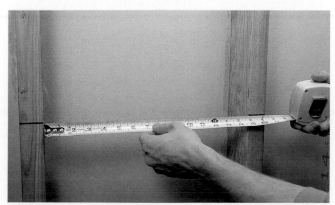

2 Measure the space between studs, and cut blocking to fit between them. If you're not sure about the exact height, use a wide board.

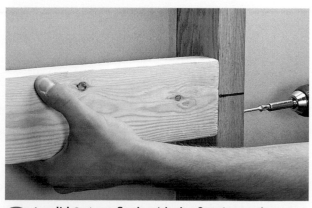

3 A solid 2x4 set flush with the framing and screwed through adjacent studs provides a solid backup for surface-mounted hardware.

Tile Basics

ROOM PREP: BATHROOMS

REMOVING A SINK

Although you can tile up to or over a sink edge, in most cases you need to remove the unit before tiling the counter. Most sinks will release after you unscrew the small fittings below the counter that keep it in place. You also may have to slice through a layer of caulk under the sink lip. The job can get a bit more complicated when you need to disconnect the water supply and drainpipes. The first step, of course, is to cut off the water supply. Then you can go to work on the sink drain, the fixture mountings, and the trap.

Balky Joints. Although many new drain fittings have a wide flange and are designed to be turned only hand-tight, you may need a Stilson wrench to release old connections.

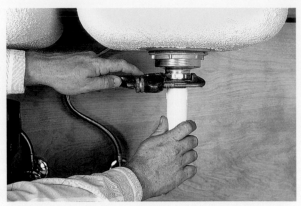

1 Even with plastic piping, the connection to the drain tailpiece is usually metal. You need to loosen it using a wrench.

REMOVING A TOILET

It's not a pleasant job, to be sure. But if you skip the sometimes difficult process of removing the toilet, you may find that tiling up to the base causes problems. First, you'll have to trim tiles around the edges, some of which are curved. Second, the grout seam may not last because the connection is subject to stress. Instead, remove the unit so that you can extend tile under the base.

A New Wax Seal. You'll find that the hidden connection between the toilet and the drain is sealed with a wax ring. Don't try to reuse the existing ring. Scrape away the old material around the drain, and install a new one before setting the fixture back in place.

1 Start by turning off the water at the cutoff valve. Then loosen the holding nut, and release the supply pipe. You can leave it attached to the fixture.

SANITARY SILLS

There are many ways to make a transition between slightly different floor levels—for example, where new plywood or backer board and tile raises the floor in a bathroom. Some sills cover the tile edge, so you install them after the job. In bathrooms, it's customary to install a piece of marble, called a sanitary sill. Because it often starts off the main field and controls the layout, you should install this sill before tiling. It's also wise to try a dry run, setting down samples of underlayment and tile to determine how different elements will join the sill.

Setting Marble. Use pressure or a rubber mallet to set the sill. Marble is brittle and can crack easily under excessive force or sharp blows.

1 You may need to strip back flooring, such as ³/₄-in. oak, to install a marble sill. To prevent cracking, the subfloor should be flat and smooth.

2 Use a long-handled basin wrench to reach behind a sink and unscrew fittings that connect the water lines to the faucet fixture.

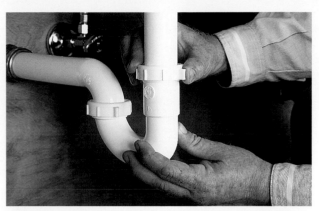

3 If you have trouble disconnecting the tailpiece, try loosening the drain line at the trap. Plug the hole temporarily to stop sewer gas from escaping.

2 After you drain the holding tank and bowl, remove the cover caps along the base rim, and unscrew the nuts holding the fixture to the drain.

3 Scrape away old wax around the drain flange. You may want to temporarily stuff up the drain to keep sewer gas from escaping.

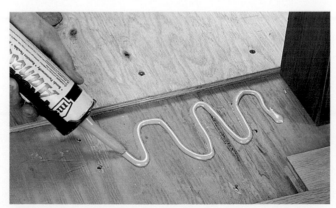

2 Spread a liberal bead of adhesive over the subfloor. If you use a synthetic sill, check the manufacturer's recommendation for adhesive.

3 Hand pressure is usually enough to set the sill in adhesive. If you need to make small adjustments, use a rubber mallet.

Tile Basics

INSTALLING LIGHTS AND SWITCHES

In any room where you plan to tile, it pays to install wiring ahead of time as part of the room preparation. Fishing cable through framing and cutting into walls is likely to disrupt tile and grout seams if you do this work later on. Also, you can plan ahead so that outlets and switches fall evenly in the tile grid. Or you may be able to locate a kitchen switch box, for example, in a strip of existing drywall above the tiled backsplash.

Safety. Remember to cut electrical power to the circuit you are working on, and test exposed wire leads to be doubly sure the power is off. If in doubt about electrical codes and practices, leave this work to a licensed electrician.

1 Often you can take power for a kitchen light from a nearby fixture box. In this case, it's in the floor framing just below the kitchen.

REMOVING OLD VINYL

Many kitchens have a utilitarian floor made of vinyl that's considerably less expensive than tile. When you upgrade, it's wise to peel away the old material. (If you use a heat gun, bear in mind that some reach very high temperatures.) Resilient flooring generally does not provide the kind of rigid support that tile and grout requires. Also, the sheet flooring may have been installed to cover up problems that you need to fix before tiling.

Adhesive on Drywall. Take the extra time to reheat and scrape away old adhesive left after you remove the base. If you take the base along with chunks of drywall, you'll have to do a lot of repair work to provide a flat surface for the new tile.

1 To minimize repair work on the drywall surface, use a heat gun (or a hair dryer in a pinch) to loosen the vinyl adhesive.

TILING TO WOOD TRIM

If you are working in existing spaces, you may be able to remove just the quarter-round or other trim strips along baseboards, and reinstall them after tiling. Casings around doors are more difficult to deal with because they generally protrude more into the room. There are two basic options. One is to slice off just enough of the bottom of the casing to allow your tile to slip in underneath. The other is to butt the tile to the casing, and cut it to match the contour of the trim. This can be very time consuming on complex molding.

Planning Thickness. Start the cut with several backward strokes. Then cut back and forth, keeping the blade flat on the stack of materials.

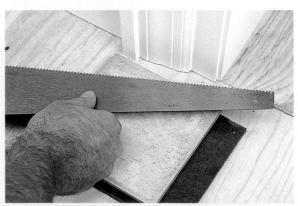

1 To make room for new tile under existing trim, use a piece of underlayment and a full tile as a depth guide for your saw.

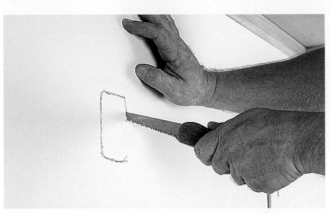

2 After securing connections with wire connectors and closing the box, mark and cut the opening for the light switch under the cabinets.

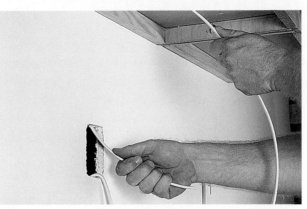

3 You can fish the power leg up through the wall framing and the switch leg down from an opening in the back of the cabinets.

2 As the adhesive bond loosens, use a drywall knife to pry the base away from the wall. You may need to work on one small section at a time.

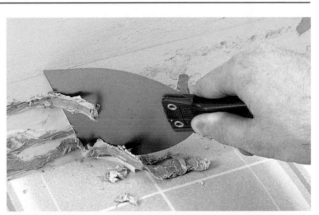

3 Reheat the remaining adhesive, if necessary, and scrape away any raised ribs. Thin deposits will be covered over with tile adhesive.

2 To butt tile against existing trim, copy the outline with a contour gauge. Small pins match the outline when you press it against the molding.

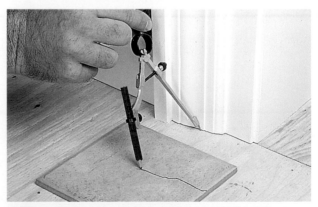

3 Another option is to mark the butt tile with a compass, scribing the cut. To be accurate, keep the pin end and the pencil end parallel as you mark.

Tile Basics

PATTERNS AND WORKING LINES

There are many ways to set tiles. For example, you can start with full-size tiles at the most visible part of a room, such as the doorway, and leave partial tiles or irregular cuts for an out-of-the-way wall. Most often, the best layout approach is to center the main field of full tiles in the area, and adjust the field to leave partial tiles that are about the same size around the edges.

Basic Tile Patterns

Whether you combine different sizes of tile or stick to a basic grid, there are several basic patterns.

Jack-on-Jack. This is the most straightforward way to install tile: in a grid with tiles stacked one on top of the other. The grout seams line up vertically and horizontally. Trimming is easy because the tiles are square or rectangular like the shapes of floors and walls.

Diagonal Jack-on-Jack. This pattern is basic jack-on-jack rotated 45 degrees. The grout lines run on a diagonal. The diamond effect of this pattern has a drawback, though. Wherever the corners of tiles meet a floor or wall, you have to trim off the point to create a horizontal or vertical edge. This system often looks best in a frame of square tiles.

Running Bond. This system adjusts the basic jack-on-jack by setting the center of full tiles over the grout seam in the course below. The offset creates a less defined edge than a squared-up grid, which can help to deemphasize irregular border cuts.

Establishing Working Lines

Once the pattern is established, the tile is selected, and the surface is prepared, you need to plan out working lines that will help you position the tiles. Generally you make these lines by snapping the chalk-laden string from a chalk-line box. Instead of snapping two lines close together, one line is centered in the grout joint.

Lines for a Square-Cornered Room. If the room is relatively square, the standard approach is to snap wall-to-wall chalk lines that cross in the center. Starting at the intersection, either dry-lay a row of tiles along each working line, or use a layout stick to determine where cut tiles are needed and what size they will be. Be sure to include the width of grout joints. If a row of partial tiles along one wall is less than half a tile wide, reposition the tiles so that the cut row is half a tile or wider. If the layout results in a narrow row of cut tiles, make the grout joints a bit wider to eliminate that row. If the last tile against the wall is almost the width of a full tile, make all the grout joints a bit narrower. That way you can fit a full row of tiles in the space.

WORKING-LINE OPTIONS

Square-Cornered Room

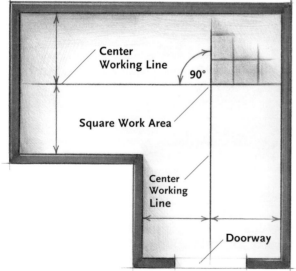

Center Working Line

90°

Square Work Area

Center Working Line

Doorway

Out-of-Square Room

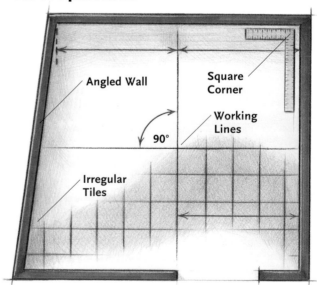

Angled Wall

Square Corner

Working Lines

90°

Irregular Tiles

Lines for an Out-of-Square Room. If the room is out-of-square, one approach is to align tile with the most prominent wall, and make irregular cuts as needed against the other walls. To determine which corner is most square, place a tile tightly against the walls in each corner of the room. Project chalk lines from the outside corner of each tile in both directions. Then check the intersections of the chalk lines at each corner for square, and choose the one that is closest to 90 degrees. Then try a dry layout. You may need to lay out a row of tiles or use a layout stick in several locations because cut tiles may work on one end of a wall but not the other.

Lines for an L-Shaped Room. Divide the room into two sections, and snap layout lines. Adjust the lines so that all intersections are at 90 degrees. Adjust lines as necessary so that cut tiles around the room's perimeter will be larger than half a tile.

Lines for an Adjoining Room. When you extend the tile field into an adjoining room, be sure to line up the grout lines. If the doorway or pass-through is wide, try to center the tiles so that cut tiles on each side are of the same width. But check to see how this arrangement effects the overall layout where tiles meet the walls.

If you are using large tiles, it helps to use additional working lines to ensure that the grout joints align properly and are of approximately the same width. Typically, you add these extra lines in a grid. Each square in the grid can contain four, six, or nine tiles with the lines representing the middle of the grout joints. Fill in one block at a time, adjusting the tiles for evenly spaced grout line.

Lines for a Diagonal Layout. When you lay tiles diagonally, you need a second set of working lines. From the intersection of the original working lines (A below), measure out an equal distance along any three of the lines (B), and drive a nail at these points. Hook the end of a measuring tape to one of the nails, and hold a pencil against the tape at a distance equal to that between the nails and center point. Use the tape and pencil as a compass to scribe two sets of arcs on the floor (C). This will provide points along the 45-degree diagonal.

Your diagonal lines will line up with grout joints between tiles. Ideally, the original lines that are square in the room should slice through the corners of the tiles. You may need to adjust the working lines to achieve the best pattern of partial tiles at all four walls. (This is where the dry layout comes into play again.) When setting the tiles, fill in one quadrant at a time.

You may also need additional working lines if you are laying unusually shaped tiles. With an interlocking shape such as an ogee that does not have fully square sides, you can snap lines as a guide for the end points or other prominent edges of the tile.

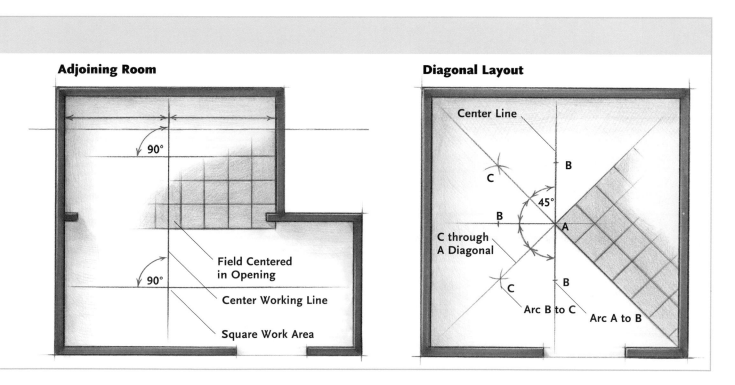

Adjoining Room

90°

90°

Field Centered in Opening

Center Working Line

Square Work Area

Diagonal Layout

Center Line

B

C

45°

B

A

C through A Diagonal

C

B

Arc B to C

Arc A to B

tools and materials 2

IF YOU ARE AN ACTIVE DO-IT-YOURSELFER, you probably own many of the tools you'll need for tile work. You may want to buy a few specialized tile tools, such as a wet saw, but you can also rent them. Shop for quality in tools you will use often. Don't pay for heavy-duty contractor tools you'll use occasionally. Buy tools that are in the ballpark of your skill level, with features you can really use. Stick with basic tools designed to do one job well. Avoid multipurpose gimmick tools. If in doubt, avoid the most- and least-expensive models. The top end often has more capacity than you need, and the bottom end often has fundamental flaws.

LAYOUT AND PREP TOOLS

You may already have most of the tools needed to lay out a tile project. To square up and level the job, you'll use a level and a square, of course, but you'll also need a chalk-line box to snap guidelines. Where measuring is concerned, take your pick: a measuring tape or a folding carpenter's rule. Not much hammering is involved in tile work, but you may need a hammer (and many other basic tools) to prepare the site—for example, if you have to lay new plywood subflooring. You may even need a pipe wrench if you need to remove kitchen or bathroom fixtures.

Remember that tile is hard, and chips can fly when you cut it. Wear safety glasses or goggles to protect your eyes. Because most cutting and grinding procedures create fine dust that can irritate your lungs, wear a respirator or at least a mask during jobs that produce dust. You may also want to invest in a set of knee pads, particularly if you are planning to tile a floor.

▲
A—rubber gloves
B—work gloves
C—knee pads
D—safety glasses
E—safety goggles
F—particle mask
G—respirator
H—ear protectors

◄ **A**—portable drill
B—level
C—circular saw
D—framing square
E—pipe wrench
F—backer-board cutting tool
G—chalk-line box
H—combination square
I—6-in. drywall taping knife
J—measuring tape
K—hammer
L—utility knife
M—sandpaper
N—masonry chisel
O—carpenter's pencil
P—screwdriver
Q—putty knife
R—utility saw

CUTTING TOOLS

To make straight cuts in some glazed tile, all you need is a conventional glass cutter, a metal straightedge, and a length of coat-hanger wire or thin dowel. Simply score the glazed surface of the tile with the cutter guided along the straightedge. Then place the tile on the wire or dowel with the score mark centered directly above it, and press down on both sides of the tile to snap it.

But there are a few improvements that you can easily make on this somewhat simple approach. The most basic is using a snap tile cutter, also called a guillotine cutter because the tool scores and snaps tile. If you have many straight cuts to make, a snap cutter will speed things along considerably and produce cleaner cuts. (Snap cutters are available at tool-rental shops.)

These tools come in several sizes and variations, but most consist of a metal frame that holds the tile in position and a carbide-tipped blade or wheel that travels along a guide rod, ensuring a square cut. Most also have a built-in ridge and a handle that you use to snap

the tile once it's scored. After positioning the tile, draw the carbide blade or wheel across the surface to score it. Then press down on the handle until the tile snaps. (See "Using a Snap Tile Cutter," page 46.)

Most snap cutters will not work on large, thick tiles, such as quarry tile or pavers. If you have just a few of these tiles to cut, use this variation of the score-and-snap method. Fit a hacksaw with a carbide-grit blade; then cut a groove about $\frac{1}{16}$ inch deep in the face of the tile. (Very thick tiles may require a second cut on the back to get a clean snap.) Then set the tile over a wood dowel or heavy wire, and press down sharply to snap. This system will work but should be reserved for only one or two problem cuts. If you have many tiles proving troublesome to cut in a snap cutter, use a wet saw.

This tool is also the best bet (on any kind of tile) if you have many irregular cuts to make. A wet saw is basically a stationary circular saw with a water-cooled carbide-grit blade. (You can rent one for the job at a tool-rental shop.) The saw component stays put, and you guide the tile into it on a sliding table. (See page 46, "Using a Wet Saw.")

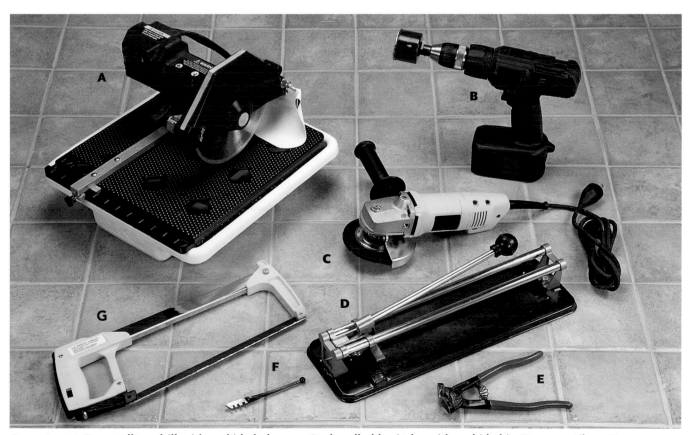

A—wet saw; **B**—cordless drill with carbide hole saw; **C**—handheld grinder with carbide bit; **D**—snap tile cutter; **E**—tile nippers; **F**—glass cutter; **G**—hacksaw with carbide blade

smart tip

USING A SNAP TILE CUTTER

A SNAP CUTTER MAKES QUICK WORK OF SQUARE CUTS. POSITION THE TILE AGAINST THE STOP AT THE HEAD OF THE TOOL, AND DRAW THE SCORING WHEEL ACROSS THE SURFACE.

THE HANDLE ON A TYPICAL SNAP CUTTER HAS TWO FUNCTIONS. FIRST USE IT TO SCORE THE TILE. THEN PRESS DOWN TO SPLIT THE TILE ALONG THE SCORE LINE.

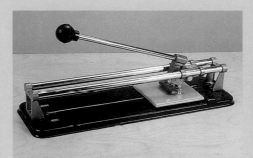

USING A WET SAW

BE SURE TO WEAR SAFETY GLASSES when using a wet saw. Also pay particular attention to how you feed the tile into the blade. The tile should be firmly seated on the platform, and you should ease it into the blade, making sure that your fingers stay clear.

TOOLS & MATERIALS

▎Wet saw (rentable)

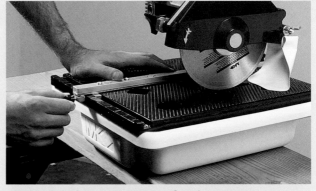

1 A typical wet saw comes fitted to a water reservoir. A circulating system feeds a stream of water onto the cutting area to lubricate the blade.

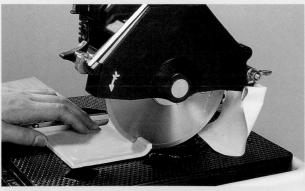

2 On a wet saw, you feed the work into the blade instead of pulling the blade into the work. You need to hold the tile securely on the cutting table.

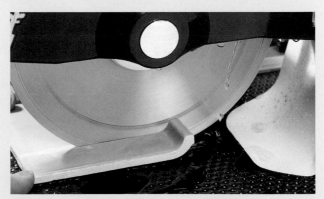

3 The fine-toothed blade slices through tile more slowly than a wood blade cuts through lumber. The saw can handle coves and other shapes.

Cutting Irregular Shapes

There are bound to be spots where you can't use a full tile or a partial tile trimmed with a snap cutter. In some cases, you can get by using a straight-cutting tool to slice off a corner. For example, if you are tiling near a baseboard convector you may be able to avoid a feed pipe coming through the floor by trimming off a corner of a tile with a snap cutter. The tile may not close up neatly around the pipe, but that won't matter if the cut is concealed by the convector cover.

In many cases, a tile nipper will do the job. The trick is to be patient and take small bites, sometimes as small as 1/8 inch. Once you get the knack of nibbling away at tiles without cracking them, you'll find that it doesn't take long to fit a tile against a pipe.

Where a pipe will protrude through a tile, instead of nicking its edge, another option is to fit your power drill with a masonry hole saw—a tubular bit with cutting teeth. It's wise to test out a hole-saw cut on scrap tile. You need to hold the drill steady and keep the bit plumb, particularly as you start the cut. The result is a neat hole that allows for grout or caulk. Of course, this approach will work only if you can cut or disconnect the pipe in order to slip the tile in position.

You can also use a wet saw to make irregular cutouts. This tool is particularly handy if you need to fit a tile against molding or any surface with an intricate shape. The idea is to make a series of closely spaced parallel cuts to the required depths. Then break out the thin slices of tile standing between saw kerfs.

USING TILE NIPPERS

IF YOU HAVEN'T USED THIS TOOL BEFORE, expect to break a few tiles before you get the hang of it. If you need to fit a tile around part of a pipe or other obstruction, first mark your cut line. Then start taking very small bites with the teeth of the nipper. Big bites are likely to break the tile beyond your cut lines.

TOOLS & MATERIALS

▌Nippers

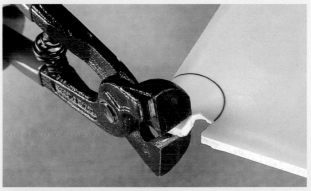

1 Start your cuts by taking very small bites along the edge of the tile. You should work up to your cut marks gradually, which takes patience.

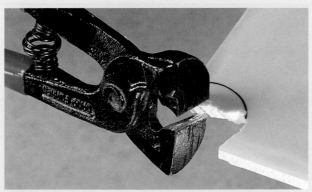

2 You can take slightly larger bites once the area is more defined. It pays to practice on some scrap tiles—and plan for extra waste just in case.

3 The teeth of a nipper will leave a slightly ragged edge. Where appearance counts, you may want to clean up the nipped edges with a file.

SPREADING ADHESIVE

USING A NOTCHED TROWEL makes it easy to spread adhesive. You can sweep the blade back and forth and be certain that you are leaving the right amount of adhesive. Just be sure that the depth of the notches on the trowel matches the recommendation of the adhesive manufacturer.

TOOLS & MATERIALS

▮ Notched trowel
▮ Tile adhesive

1 Spread adhesive on one section of the floor at a time, not the entire surface, to give yourself some working room on the subfloor surface.

2 Trowel notches produce evenly spaced ribs of adhesive that are the same size. Embed the tiles in the ribs with a slight twist for a secure bond.

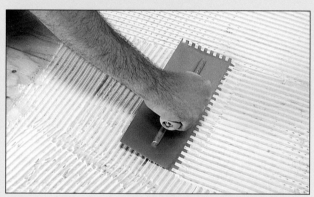

3 You can use a sweeping stroke over large areas. First spread out a pile of adhesive before creating the ridges with the toothed edge.

SETTING TOOLS AND MATERIALS

To set tile, you'll need tools for mixing and spreading adhesive and for embedding and leveling the tiles. You will also need a way to maintain even grout lines. Wall tiles often have spacing nubs molded into their sides. Some pros are so experienced that they can do the job by eye. But most do-it-yourselfers use plastic spacers.

Mixing and Spreading Adhesive

You should use premixed adhesive on thinset work, and mix your own only in special cases. If you are tackling a thickset mortar job and mixing large amounts of cement-based adhesive, you will need a mason's hoe and wheelbarrow or a large sheet-metal cement-mixing barge. To mix powdered grout, use a bucket and a mortar-mixing paddle or paint mixer chucked in an electric drill. (Use the mixer at a slow speed, 300 rpm or less.)

In most cases, a notched trowel is all you need to apply adhesive. Typically, only one side and one end of the trowel is notched. This allows you to use the flat side to spread the adhesive initially and the notched side to comb out the mix and create even ribs.

Trowels come with various-size square or V-shaped notches for spreading different adhesives for different tiles. The size is specified by the tile or adhesive manufacturer. You may need other mason's tools, such as floats, to level and finish thickset mortar beds.

EMBEDDING TILES

YOU NEED ONLY MODERATE PRESSURE over ribs of tile adhesive to create a good bond. But tapping on a padded block that reaches over several tiles may be necessary to be sure that the tiles are flush.

TOOLS & MATERIALS

▌ Hammer (or rubber mallet)
▌ Wood block
▌ Cushioned cover for block
▌ Tile spacers

1 Moderate pressure combined with a slight side-to-side motion is usually enough to bond the tile with the adhesive.

2 Small plastic spacers help to maintain even grout seams as you work tiles into position. You usually remove spacers before grouting.

3 Use a piece of 2x4 wrapped in a carpet scrap to even out the tile surface, if necessary.

Tile Spacers

To ensure even spacing for grout joints, some tiles (typically wall tiles) have small spacing nubs molded into the edges. When you set two of these tiles together, the nubs match up and create a gap for grout. If the tiles you are using do not have nubs, there are several ways to keep an even layout.

The most reliable system is to set molded plastic spacers in the gaps. These cross-shaped fittings are available in many sizes (generally from $\frac{1}{32}$ to $\frac{1}{2}$ inch), so you can use them on small tiles with narrow grout lines and on large tiles with thick grout lines.

Follow the tile manufacturer's recommendations about which size and type to use. Some can be set flat, left in place, and covered with grout. Many types are set vertically and removed after the tile sets but before you grout.

On countertops, you can mark the centers of the grout lines, attach 6d finishing nails at each end, and stretch dampened cotton cord between them. On floors with wide grout joints, you may want to use wooden battens as spacers between tiles.

Embedding and Leveling Tiles

To assist in bedding tiles into adhesive, you may want to use a hammer or rubber mallet and a bedding block. To make a bedding block, cut a wood block large enough to cover several tiles at once, and cover it with heavy fabric or scrap carpet. You may need a metal straightedge to periodically make sure that the tiles are even and level and that the grout joints remain aligned.

Tools and Materials

FINISHING TOOLS

Grout Tools

To apply grout, the typical procedure is to spread a liberal amount across the tile surface, working on a diagonal to the joints with a rubber float or squeegee. With repeated passes you gradually force grout into the joints.

You can also use a grout bag. It's similar to a pastry bag and has a small fitting on one end to which you can attach nozzles of different sizes to control the amount of grout applied to the joint. After filling the bag, squeeze it to lay a bead of grout directly into the joint. Grout bags work well in situations where cleaning excess grout off the tile surface would be difficult or where the grout might stain the tile surface.

Drawbacks to using the bag include problems with applying a fast-setting grout and mixing this grout to a usable consistency. If the grout is too thin and watery, it won't bond well. If you use the more common method of grouting with a float, it may help if you use a squeegee to clear excess grout off the surface. Then, as the grout dries, you'll need a sponge or two to remove the grout haze. Rinse the sponge regularly in clean water, and make several passes.

Striking and Jointing Tools

Although most grout is left flush (or nearly flush) to make tile surfaces easier to clean, you may want to strike the grout joints to create a particular pattern. You can buy special striking tools or simply run down the joints with a wooden stick or small tool handle.

Finally, you may need a caulking gun to install polyurethane or silicone caulk in joints where the tile meets dissimilar materials—for example, where wall tiles meet the rim of a tub. Just insert the caulking tube into the gun, snip the tip of the caulking tube, and apply pressure on the gun trigger to fill the gap.

A—masonry trowel; **B**—sponge; **C**—grout sealer with applicator; **D**—bucket; **E**—grout float; **F**—grout bag; **G**—rubber mallet; **H**—scouring pad; **I**—bedding block; **J**—tile spacers; **K**—notched trowel; **L**—carbide emery cloth; **M**—grout saw; **N**—caulking gun; **O**—spacer remover

BASIC MATERIALS

Although ceramic tile can be laid over a variety of existing surfaces, there may be cases when you must install a smooth, rigid surface.

Cement Backer Board

Also called cementitious backer units, or CBUs, cement backer board is a rigid, portland cement-based panel designed for use as a substrate or underlayment for ceramic tile in wet or dry areas. Sometimes the binder material is made of fiberglass-reinforced coatings. Different types are recommended for interior floors, interior walls, and exterior walls.

Next to a thick-bed mortar installation, cement backer board is the best substrate for wet areas. Although it is not waterproof, water will not damage it. Wood, plywood, particleboard, and drywall underlayments will deteriorate when exposed to water. And because cement backer board is a rigid, dense, dimensionally stable product, it does not expand and contract as much as conventional wood subflooring and underlayment materials.

Backer board is available in several thicknesses. The most commonly used is ½-inch thick. The panels also come in several widths, but are usually 4 × 4 or 3 × 5 feet.

You install CBUs basically the same way you install drywall. The panels are a bit trickier to cut, but you can score and snap the panels to get a clean edge. Because CBUs are heavy and rigid, install them directly over wall studs using corrosion-resistant nails or screws.

Backer board is also fireproof, so you can use it in place of asbestos board as an insulating material for woodstove surrounds. And using it in conjunction with tile may allow reduced clearances between the stove and wall. Check the manufacturer's directions and local building codes to be sure of clearances at combustion sources.

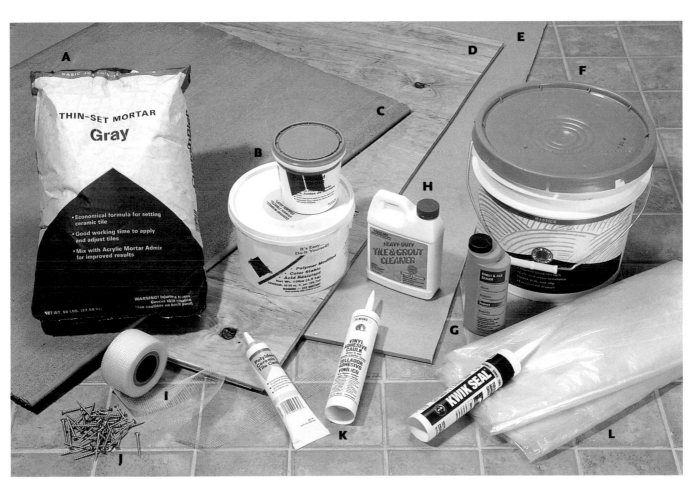

A—thinset mortar mix; B—premixed tile grouts; C—cement backer board; D—plywood; E—greenboard; F—tile mastic; G—tile & grout sealer; H—tile and grout cleaner; I—fiberglass mesh tape; J—galvanized screws; K—caulking products; L—4-mil plastic film (waterproof membrane)

EXPANSION JOINTS

PLACE EXPANSION JOINTS around installations where tile abuts a different material. When tiling a floor, simply stop the tile and underlayment about ¼ inch short of the wall, and fill the joint with a flexible silicone caulk. Prefabricated PVC corner expansion joints are also available. On interior walls and floors, special joints are usually not needed within the tile field itself. Filling all joints between field tiles with the appropriate grout should provide the proper cohesive bond.

YOU MAY NEED CONTROL JOINTS on large patios, where the joints are needed about every 16 feet. You make control joints by pulling a special tool across the uncured concrete, leaving a groove. Designed to be the weak link in the concrete slab, control joints should crack. These joints in the substrate are generally carried up through the grout lines between the surface tiles. You can fill these joints with a compressible foam rod topped by urethane caulk instead of a traditional grout.

INTERIOR APPLICATION

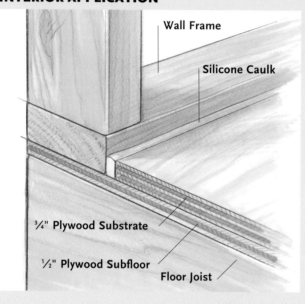

Wall Frame
Silicone Caulk
¾" Plywood Substrate
½" Plywood Subfloor
Floor Joist

EXTERIOR APPLICATION

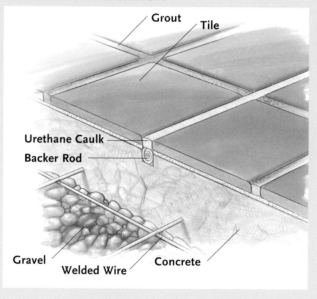

Grout
Tile
Urethane Caulk
Backer Rod
Gravel
Welded Wire
Concrete

WATERPROOF AND ISOLATION MEMBRANES

To make a tile job durable, you need to keep out water, which can weaken the bond between the tile and underlayment and eventually damage the underlayment and framing beneath. In a wet area such as a tub surround, waterproof membranes are recommended between the studs and the substrate to prevent this kind of damage.

It's tempting sometimes to use waterproof membranes when you want to install tile over concrete floors that are subject to rising water from below. But the best plan in such cases is to deal with whatever is causing the problem, such as faulty drainage. Tar paper or building felt have long been used as moisture-resistant membranes. Other types include chlorinated polyethylene (generally called CPE) and combination liquid and fabric membranes. Make sure the membrane is compatible with the setting material.

Isolation membranes separate tile from the underlayment to compensate for differences in expansion and contraction rates. Typically, they consist of chlorinated polyethylene sheets laminated between the tile and substrate. You may need an isolation membrane if the existing underlayment shows signs of excessive movement. Signs include cracks in masonry and cracks at joints where two different subflooring materials meet. If you suspect excessive seasonal movement or a weak substructure, it's best to seek professional advice.

MORTAR AND ADHESIVES

The traditional setting method is to lay the tiles directly in a bed of wet portland cement mortar. It's still used in some situations—for example, if you need to create a sloping floor in a shower enclosure. But most tile work is done with thinset adhesive.

Thickset

Installing thick-bed mortar requires considerable experience. Some tile-setters lay down the mortar bed, smooth it, allow it to cure, and then set the tiles over the bed with a bond coat of cement adhesive. In any case, the job is best left to a professional.

Thinset

There are many thinset adhesives on the market. A tile dealer can recommend the best adhesive for the job, but you will probably wind up using a cement-based adhesive (mortar) or an organic mastic adhesive, and in some cases an epoxy-based mortar.

Portland Cement Mortars

These adhesives are actually forms of cement-based mortar, although they should not be confused with the portland cement mortar used for thick-bed installations. Most of these nonflammable, thinset mortars come in powder form. Some must be mixed with sand before use. Some come as premixed liquids. Powdered forms are mixed with water or a liquid latex additive.

Dry-Set Mortars

These are the most common adhesives, generally sold in powder form and mixed with water. Highly resistant to impact, dry-set mortar can be cleaned up easily with water. Once cured, this mortar is not affected by prolonged contact with water, so it can be used in wet installations.

A typical installation has a layer about $3/32$ inch thick. The material will cover and level minor surface irregularities, but it is not intended for leveling very rough surfaces.

Dry-set mortars adhere well to a variety of substrate materials, including relatively smooth masonry, insulation board, drywall, and cement backer board. Some types are suitable for use over plywood. Check the label for appropriate applications.

SETTING ALTERNATIVES

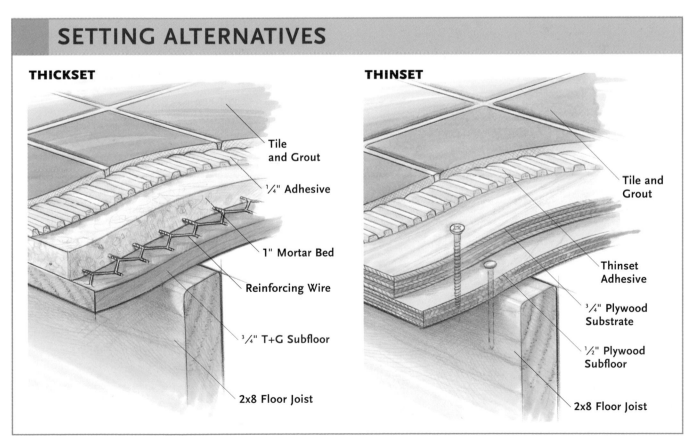

THICKSET

Tile and Grout
$1/4$" Adhesive
1" Mortar Bed
Reinforcing Wire
$3/4$" T+G Subfloor
2x8 Floor Joist

THINSET

Tile and Grout
Thinset Adhesive
$3/4$" Plywood Substrate
$1/2$" Plywood Subfloor
2x8 Floor Joist

smart tip

SEALING GROUT

GLAZED TILES HAVE GREAT RESISTANCE TO DIRT, MOLD, AND MILDEW. BUT THE GROUT BETWEEN TILES CAN BECOME A CHRONIC CLEANING PROBLEM UNLESS YOU PROTECT IT WITH A SEALER. MILDEW CAN BE REMOVED USING BLEACH. GROUND-IN DIRT ON FLOORS AND SUCH MAY BE IMPOSSIBLE TO REMOVE. HERE YOU SHOULD USE DARK GROUTS.

General cleaning may not take care of stains in grout. Try to scrub the grout using a brush (even an old toothbrush) with a concentrated cleaner and/or bleach.

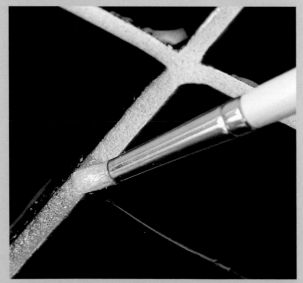

To protect grout seams in areas that are chronically damp or exposed to traffic, use a small brush to coat cleaned grout with a liberal coat of liquid silicone sealer.

Latex Portland Cement Mortars

These mortars are a mixture of portland cement, sand, and a liquid latex additive. They have the same basic applications as dry-set mortars, although they have higher compressive and bond strengths and greater flexibility. Latex portland cement mortars cost a bit more than the dry-set kind, but they perform better.

Organic Mastic Adhesives

Although most of these adhesives do not have the bond strength or leveling properties of thinsets, they are the easiest to apply. Most brands cannot be used in wet installations or near heat sources, however. (Organic adhesives generally should not be used in areas with temperatures over 140 degrees F.) Suitable backings include drywall, smooth plaster or mortar, plywood, tile backer board, and smooth, dry concrete. Organic mastics are water-based.

Epoxy-Based Mortars

Epoxies are not used much by do-it-yourselfers because they are more expensive and harder to apply than other adhesives. You must mix the resin and hardener to exact proportions and apply them at the correct temperature to ensure the right setting time and pot life. Epoxy mortars are useful when you need a high degree of bond strength or when the tiled surface will receive a high degree of physical or chemical wear. They will adhere to just about any substrate material.

GROUTS AND SEALERS

Grouts

Tile grouts fall into two basic categories: cement-based grout and epoxy grout. Don't confuse grouts used for tiling with caulks, which are used for filling gaps between building materials. For example, silicone caulk is used at joints where tile meets other surfaces. And because silicone is highly flexible, you can use it instead of grout at tiled corners and edges where movement in the substructure would crack ordinary grout joints.

Cement-Based Grouts. These grouts have a base of portland cement, but they differ in the types of additives they contain. Coloring pigments are available for many of them, although precolored grouts also are sold.

Most cement-based grouts come in powdered form to which water or liquid latex is added. They are available sanded and unsanded. Unsanded grout is used on joints

⅛ inch or less. Some grouts are premixed, but they are usually the most expensive as well. Cement-based grouts include commercial portland cement, dry-set, and latex portland cement grouts.

Portland Cement Grout. A mixture of portland cement and other ingredients, this grout produces a dense, uniformly colored material. Like all cement-based mortars, it is resistant to water but not completely waterproof or stain proof, so it generally requires a sealer. Commercial portland cement grouts are formulated for use with thick-bed portland cement mortar installations. With these, you need to soak the tiles in water. These grouts also require damp-curing to prevent shrinking and cracking.

Dry-Set Grout. This type of portland cement grout contains additives that increase water-retention. They allow you to grout tiles without presoaking them and without damp-curing the grout once applied. If you are grouting the tiles on a hot, dry day, the grout might dry out so quickly that it will shrink, requiring you to presoak tiles and damp-cure the grout joints anyway.

Latex Portland Cement Grout. This can be any of the preceding grout types that have been mixed with powdered latex and water, or with liquid latex instead of water. This versatile grout is somewhat stronger and more flexible than latex cement mortar.

Epoxy Grout. This grout contains an epoxy resin and hardener, giving it a high degree of chemical resistance, bond strength, and impact resistance. It is the most expensive grout, and therefore usually confined to commercial applications where chemical resistance is required. Epoxy grout generally flows more easily than standard grout and is somewhat more difficult to apply. If your tiles are more than ½ inch thick and the grout joints are less than ¼ inch wide, the grout may not penetrate.

Sealers

Clear liquid tile and grout sealers provide protection against stains and, to some extent, against water penetration at grout joints. Their application is the final step in tile installation. Although glazed tiles themselves do not require a sealer, the porous cement-based grout joints usually do. Different formulations are available for different types of tile and grout in various applications. Sealers generally require reapplication every one to two years to maintain protection. But they can reduce the formation of mold and mildew in grouted joints.

GROUT TYPES

Tile/Application	Commercial Portland Cement		Sand Portland Cement	Dry-Set	Latex Portland Cement (1)	Epoxy (2, 3)	Silicone or Urethane (4)	Modified Epoxy Emulsion (1, 3)
	Walls	Floors	Walls & Floors	Walls & Floors				
Glazed Wall Tile (More than 7% absorption)		✓			✓	✓		✓
Ceramic Mosaic Tile	✓	✓	✓	✓	✓	✓	✓	✓
Quarry, Paver, and Packing House Tile	✓	✓	✓			✓		✓
Dry or Limited Water Exposure	✓	✓	✓	✓	✓	✓	✓	✓
Wet Areas	✓	✓	✓	✓	✓	✓	✓	✓
Exteriors	✓	✓	✓	✓	✓(5)	✓(5)		✓(5)
Stain Resistance (6)	D	C	E	D	B	A	A	B
Crack Resistance (6)	D	D	E	D	C	B	A Flexible	C
Colorability (6)	B	B	C	B	B	B	Restricted	B

(1) Special cleaning procedures and materials needed.
(2) Mainly used for chemical-resistant properties.
(3) Epoxies are recommended for prolonged temperatures up to 140°F, high-temperature-resistant epoxies up to 350°F.
(4) Special tools needed for proper application. Silicone and urethane are used when installing pregrouted ceramic tile sheets. Silicone grout should not be used on kitchen countertops or other food-preparation surfaces.
(5) Follow manufacturer's directions.
(6) Five performance ratings—best to minimal (A B C D E).

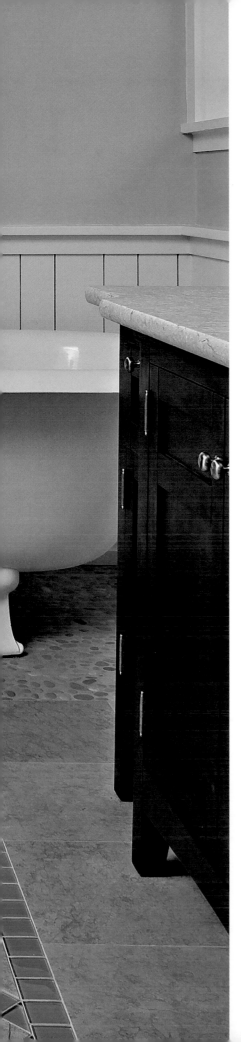

tiling floors

3

CERAMIC AND STONE TILES provide a durable surface that will complement practically any room and its furnishings. Bear in mind, though, that tile can be hard and cold underfoot. That's why it is not often used in bedrooms or living rooms and reserved mainly for kitchens, bathrooms, and entry halls.

Before you lay a ceramic- or stone-tile floor, the existing floor must be strong and rigid enough to support the added weight of the tile. Strength is rarely a problem, but you may need to reinforce joists or add extra subflooring (or both) to make the floor rigid so that it does not flex.

DESIGN BASICS

Although the subject of design involves numerous considerations—and is largely a matter of personal taste—a few basic principles always apply.

When choosing a tile for your floor, you need to consider five elements: size, shape, color, texture, and pattern. Together, all five elements determine the overall visual effect you are trying to achieve. The first four elements apply to the tile you select. The last element, pattern, is controlled both by the tile itself and by the way they are arranged on the floor.

Size

As a general rule, tile size has an inverse effect on rooms: small tiles make a floor look larger, and large tiles make a floor look smaller. If you're tiling a small lavatory with several twists and turns in the walls, a small, simple, and uniform tile will probably look best. If you're tiling a somewhat cavernous entry hall at the foot of a expansive two-story stairwell, 12 × 12s may help to pull the large space together.

But there is always a trade-off in design decisions. Where tile size is concerned, it involves both installation time and possible future maintenance. Because large tiles cover a lot of area, installing them is faster than it would be with small tiles. Also, there are fewer grout lines in a field of large tiles, which means less cleaning and sealing as the floor is subjected to daily wear and tear.

Shape

Because most tiles are square, this is the shape people expect to see. When you choose a different shape—hexagonal, octagonal, or ogee, for instance—or combine shapes, you immediately draw attention to the floor.

Color

Dark colors tend to make a space look smaller, while lighter shades generally provide a more spacious feeling. Warm terra-cotta colors suggest a rustic look, whereas black, white, and bold colors can impart a more modern appearance. Light pastels, such as pink, peach, or light blues and greens, can soften a room while lending an airy feeling. Sharply contrasting colors and patterns usually draw attention to the floor, whereas a single-color or low-contrast color scheme creates a subtle backdrop for furniture or other focal points in the room. You need to plan color schemes carefully, considering wall paint color, natural light, and other factors, to avoid conflicts with other elements in the room.

Tile size should be appropriate for the room, with larger units and size combinations reserved for large spaces.

Tile shapes (and different surface textures) can be combined to create borders and define areas.

The color and size of these bathroom floor tiles help anchor the design of the room.

Tiling Floors

Tile texture as well as size and shape can help to define walkways, entries, and other areas of a room.

Texture

The surface texture of a tile often plays a more subtle role than the other style elements. But it is an important link to the overall feeling of a room with a tiled floor. For example, handmade Mexican pavers have an uneven surface that creates a purposefully irregular, heavily textured look. Combined with color gradations within each tile, this can set a distinctly rustic style. On the other hand, machine-made pavers with a uniformly smooth surface texture and even coloring have a crisp, clean look. A highly glazed surface can seem to expand a space and brighten a room, while a matte finish often diminishes space and makes a room feel more cozy.

Pattern

The way you combine the different design elements of shape, size, and color determines the overall pattern of the floor. Consider that the pattern serves not only to add visual interest to the floor but also can underscore particular features of a room, such as its length. A strong directional pattern running lengthwise makes a room look longer and narrower, while a crossing pattern makes a room look shorter and wider. You can also use multiple patterns to define areas. For example, you might change a square grid layout in the main field into a diagonal pattern around the edge of a room or along a walkway. A pattern change can also separate spaces—at a pass-through between rooms, for example—while a continuing grid serves to draw them together. Manipulating lines of sight can also increase apparent space and create a unifying effect—for instance, when you continue tile from inside onto an outdoor patio. Generally, busy patterns decrease apparent floor size, while simple patterns enlarge it.

Grout has an impact on the design. Using a contrasting grout color will emphasize a pattern, while a matching grout color provides a more subtle effect. Remember that dark grout hides dirt better than a light color, so think twice before using white grout. If you also plan on tiling the wall, it is usually best to use one size of tile on the wall and another on the floor, especially if floors and walls are not perfectly level, square, or plumb.

Changing scale or pattern—installing what amounts to a tile baseboard, for example—will separate wall and floor grids and disguise any discrepancies where grout joints might not align. There are many types of specially shaped tiles, generally with a cove shape, that suit this purpose. Also, you can include a strip of border tiles of a contrasting color or pattern around the room perimeter to frame a pattern in the main tile field. Be sure to subtract the thickness of the cove when planning the layout of the field tiles on the floor.

Even within these basic guidelines there are so many possibilities that it pays to experiment before you decide on a final combination of elements. You can do this on your own with graph paper and colored pencils, or use the computer-imaging services available at some tile stores and home centers.

Finish

For indoor floors, you can use a glazed or unglazed tile. Glazed tiles are easier to clean, while some unglazed tiles require sealing and waxing. If you want to use an unglazed tile indoors, use a vitreous quarry tile that is at least somewhat stain resistant. In wet areas, choose a tile with a slip-resistant surface, and avoid slick, highly glazed tiles. Outdoors, unglazed tiles are often a better choice than tiles with a glazed surface, which can be slick when wet.

Also, consider investing some extra time in the job of finishing the grout, particularly in damp areas where mildew forms easily on the surface. A protective coat of clear silicone, for example, can make cleaning and maintenance much easier.

You can combine tiles of different colors, sizes, patterns, and textures into a unique design.

Tile patterns range from a subtle contrasting shade in a border to highly defined murals and mosaics.

PLANNING THE LAYOUT

A scale drawing will help you lay out and estimate the tile job. Be sure to indicate the locations of entryways and any built-in cabinets or other permanent fixtures. Measure the size of the tile itself and the width of one full grout joint, and use this as the basic measuring unit.

If you are using square tiles, plan your drawing so that each square on the graph paper represents one tile and its grout-joint measurement. The idea is to superimpose a field of tiles on an outline of the room to see how it fits.

Plan the layout so a narrow row of cut tiles does not end up in a visually conspicuous place, such as at a doorway or entry. Often, the best plan is to adjust the field so that cut tiles at opposite sides of the room will be the same size. This gives the most symmetrical look to the installation.

If you start laying tiles from the exact center of the room out toward each wall, you may end up with narrow cut tiles at both walls. To correct this, shift the original centerline, or working line, a distance equal to half a tile to the left or right. This will give you wider-cut tiles at both walls. If the tiles extend into an adjacent room, lay out both floors so that the grout joints line up through the entryways.

In short, if you plan the layout carefully in advance on paper, you will eliminate unpleasant surprises once the project is well underway.

BASIC TILE SHAPES AND PATTERNS

The most basic tile shape is a square that forms a symmetrical grid, such as 12x12 terra-cotta.

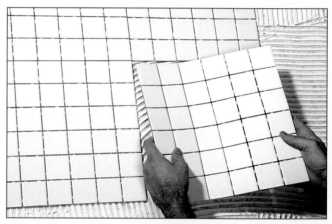

The many variations on a square include sizes you set individually and the sheet-mounted tile shown.

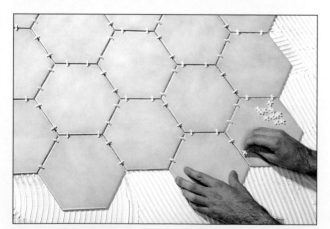

Hexagon-shaped tile creates more of an interlocked, multidirectional pattern and requires edge trimming.

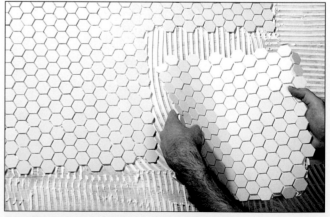

Small hexagonal tiles (and other small units) are sheet-mounted to make installation more convenient

smart tip

MAKING A LAYOUT STICK

A LAYOUT STICK WITH MARKS FOR TILE AND GROUT CAN COME IN HANDY WHEN YOU ESTABLISH WORKING LINES ON THE FLOOR. IT'S ALSO GOOD FOR SPACING TILES IF YOU DON'T USE SPACERS. THE STICK CAN BE A STRAIGHT PIECE OF 1x4 (FOR ¾-INCH TILE), CUT TO 3 OR 4 FEET IF YOU'RE WORKING IN A SMALL BATCH OR UP TO 8 FEET ON LARGER ROOMS.

IF YOU'RE USING INDIVIDUAL TILES OR TILES WITH LUGS ON THE EDGES TO CONTROL GROUT SPACING, MARK THE DIMENSIONS OF THE TILE AND JOINTS ALONG THE EDGE OF THE STICK. WITH TILE SHEETS, MARK THE SIZE OF THE SHEETS, LEAVING SPACES FOR THE JOINTS BETWEEN EACH SHEET.

Align tiles with spacers to create the proper spacing; then use a combination square to transfer marks to the layout stick.

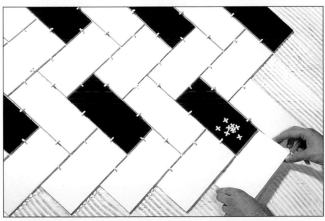

Rectangular tiles can form many patterns, from straight running bonds to basketweaves.

By combining basic shapes, such as squares and rectangles, you can create a wide variety of patterns.

Sheet-mounted tiles are available in many patterns, including random combinations of color and size.

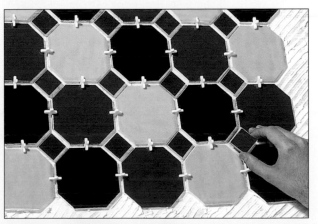

Custom combinations of different sizes, shapes, and colors are possible if you stick to stock sizes.

Tiling Floors

CHECKING THE FLOOR FOR SQUARE AND LEVEL

project

Very few room corners are exactly square, and few floors are dead level, particularly in older homes. Make minor improvements to out-of-square floors by adjusting the width of the grout joints between tiles. For out-of-level floors, you may need to shim the floor and apply a layer of plywood subflooring. But if the floor is flat, even if it isn't exactly level, you can fill all the cracks and gaps in the subflooring with floor-leveling compound.

TOOLS & MATERIALS

▌Measuring tape
▌4-ft. level and straightedge board
▌Hammer ▌Drill/driver
▌String and scrap wood blocks
▌Nails

1 Check all the inside corners of the room for square using a 3-4-5 right triangle. To do this, measure 3 ft. from the corner along one wall, and make a mark. Then measure 4 ft. from the corner along the other wall, and make a mark. Check the distance between these two marks. If it's 5 ft., the corner is square.

KNEE PADS

KNEE PADS don't qualify as essential safety equipment, but they can make the job of laying tiles on a floor a lot easier. In fact, most professionals use them. Of course, pros work on floors day in and day out, while do-it-yourselfers may tackle this kind of project only once. But if you have problems with your knees, or simply want to be more comfortable when you work, buy and use a pair of knee pads. Some products have a hard outer shell with cushioning foam on the inside. Others are made of just foam with a fabric covering. The former types are more durable, while the latter are easy to wash if they get dirty. When both types are adjusted properly, they are hardly noticeable, even when work shorts (instead of long pants) are being worn. Knee pads make roof work much more comfortable too, especially when you are installing new shingles.

Most pads strap on easily to provide a stable and padded working platform that's easy on the knees.

2 After checking for square, check the floor surface for level using a 4-ft.-long tool. Hold it on the floor next to each wall and then move it across the room in several different locations. A floor that's less than ⅛ in. out of level in 4 feet is fine, but bigger problems should be corrected.

3 When floors are out of level, check them using a longer level by placing a 4-ft. tool on top of a straight 2x4. If the floor does slope slightly in one direction, but this slope is consistent, then the floor is OK as a base for a tile floor. The subfloor being flat is more important than it being absolutely level.

4 Room corners can be square and floors can be flat and level, but you still have to check the straightness of all the walls. Severely bowed walls can make an otherwise good tile installation look sloppy. To check a wall, tack-nail a scrap block to both ends of the wall just above the floor. Then stretch a string between the two blocks.

5 Check for irregularities by sliding an identical third block between the string and the wall. If it won't fit, then the wall is bowed out. If there's a space between the block and the string, then the wall is bowed in. More than ½ in. of space in either direction will show up clearly in the floor tiles along the wall.

PREPARING THE FLOOR

Tiling is no different from other do-it-yourself projects in one important respect: much of the work involved (and often the key to a successful project) lies in the preparation. The main concern, of course, is strength. To support tile and grout without flexing enough to cause cracking, the floor must be stronger than a typical floor. It can't flex. This can make a tile floor somewhat less comfortable than a wood floor.

You can install ceramic tile directly over many existing floor coverings if the floor covering itself and the subflooring and framing below are sound. If the existing floor meets these requirements—for example, the plywood floor under carpeting—thoroughly clean the floor and, if necessary, roughen the existing surface with sandpaper to ensure a good adhesive bond. It's also a good idea to check the surface for raised seams and popped nailheads. The seams you can reduce with a block plane. The popped nails you can deal with two ways: drive them home, or pull them out and drive screws instead.

The added thickness of tile will cause a change of floor level, which will have to be dealt with at entryways where the tile meets other floor coverings. You may have to trim narrow strips off the bottoms of doors as well.

In many cases, an existing floor structure will require some tear-out and rebuilding. You may have to remove the surface flooring, strip some of the subflooring, build up some of the framing, and start from scratch. In many cases, adding one extra layer of plywood will do.

If you find that it is too difficult to remove an old floor covering, and it is in bad shape, you may be able to bury it under plywood or a backer-board underlayment and make a sound surface for new tile.

Tile floors require the support of a strong subfloor to avoid cracking.

STRENGTHENING THE SUBFLOOR

project

Remember that wooden floors are resilient; they are supposed to flex a little when you walk on them. Unfortunately, tile floors are not designed to do the same. Check your floor for any movement. Stand under the joists and press a level up against the bottom of at least three joists. Then have someone walk over the floor. If the level moves when the weight is added, your floor should be strengthened as shown here.

TOOLS & MATERIALS

▮ Drill with screwdriver bit and screws
▮ Level
▮ Extra joist (if needed)
▮ Extra floor plywood (if needed)
▮ Construction adhesive

1 Start by making sure the existing flooring is firmly attached to the floor joists. Use screws instead of nails because they hold better. Drive them into every joist, spaced about 4 in. apart. If you need to add new subflooring, stagger the joints so that the panel edges are not attached to the same joists as the panels underneath.

2 Check for sagging joists by holding a level across several joists at a time. If the level rocks over one, this means that the joist is lower than the others. A joist that sags is usually weak and therefore is a good candidate for reinforcement.

3 To reinforce a joist, attach a matching new joist to the side of the existing one. First, drive a 2x4 temporary post underneath the sagging joist until the joist is straight. Then spread construction adhesive on its side. Cut a new matching joist to length; fit it next to the sagging joist; and screw the two together in a 4-in.-sq. pattern.

BLOCKING AND BRIDGING

TO REINFORCE EXPOSED FLOOR JOISTS, add blocking or bridging. They connect the joists to each other and can prevent twisting where the bottom edges are left exposed—for example, over a crawl space. Wood blocking is solid pieces of lumber that are the same dimensions as the floor joists and set perpendicularly between the joists. Metal bridging consists of two strips of steel in an X pattern. Smaller pieces of lumber set in an X shape can also serve as bridging. Although these techniques may not be required by building codes, most people find that they add a noticeable degree of stiffness and strength.

To install metal bridging, you mount the nailing flange on the edge of the joist. You can't use these on existing floors without bending down the top flanges.

Solid blocking is easy to install because you use short lengths of lumber the same size as the floor joists. A staggered pattern allows you to end-nail each piece.

REINFORCING THE SUBFLOOR

If an existing floor feels spongy or excessively flexible when you walk on it—or if it squeaks over a large area—chances are that you will need to reinforce it. If the floor sags noticeably, you will need to level it.

Start by renailing or screwing the subfloor to the floor joists. If you have an older, board-type subfloor, you can shim individual loose boards with shingles. Gently tap shims into the space between the joists and the subfloor to prevent movement. Do not drive the shims too forcefully, or they will cause the boards to rise, resulting in a wavy floor. Then nail or screw the boards to the joists.

If several boards are loose or a sagging joist has created a springy spot in a plywood subfloor, you can add a cleat beside or between the joists in question. For example, you can cut a short piece of wood the same depth as the joists, coat its top with construction adhesive, tap it into place between joists (under the weak area), and nail it securely.

If a large area of the entire subfloor is weak because joists have settled or shifted, one approach is to strengthen the floor by adding wood blocking or metal bridging. (See above.) You can also double up weak joists. (See page 67.)

Make sure the existing subfloor material itself is in good shape. It should be sound, even, and level. In bathrooms especially, water damage to the subfloor might not be apparent until you remove the finish flooring. Replace all rotted or water-damaged wood. If a subfloor is simply wet but still sound, allow it to dry thoroughly before tiling over it. Fix the problem causing the wetness to prevent future problems.

Typically, the total thickness of the subfloor, underlayment, and existing floor material (if retained) should be at least 1⅛ inches thick. If it is not, build up the subfloor by adding an additional layer of exterior plywood (CDX or better grade), or use cement-based backer board. It is recommended for wet areas. Do not use interior-grade plywood, particleboard, or hardboard.

INSTALLING UNDERLAYMENT

project

Most contractors use cement-based backer board for both floor and wall installations. It's very stable, resistant to moisture, and is almost as easy to install as standard drywall. But plywood is a suitable substitute for use as a tile underlayment. The default choice is ½-inch-thick panels with an A-C grade rating. This means that one side (the A side) is free of voids and splits and therefore will provide a smooth stable surface for the tile.

TOOLS & MATERIALS

▮ Circular saw
▮ Drill with screwdriver bit
▮ Measuring tape
▮ Chalk-line box ▮ Plywood
▮ Galvanized screws

1 When installing new plywood, cutting 4x8 sheets is usually necessary. If space is tight, measure carefully, and make the cuts outside. If there's plenty of room to work, make the cut on-site. Measure carefully; snap a chalk line across the plywood; support the panel with 2x4s; and make the cut.

2 Once the sheet is cut, sweep away any sawdust, and make sure the floor is clean of other debris. If the panel abuts a wall, place the cut edge against the wall, leaving a space of about ¼ in., and lower the panel into place. The edges of the new panel should be staggered over the joints of the panels below.

3 Locate the position of the joists below the panel, and snap chalk lines to indicate where they are. Then attach the underlayment panels using galvanized screws that are long enough to reach at least 1 in. into the joists. Space the screws 4 to 6 in. apart, and drive the screwheads slightly below the surface of the plywood.

CHECKING FOR MOISTURE

DAMPNESS ON A CONCRETE FLOOR can be result of simple condensation, which is not a significant problem. But it can also be coming up through the slab from the ground below. This is a more serious problem because over time it can undermine the adhesion between the tile and the concrete floor. This simple test will show where the moisture is coming from. Before giving it a try, be sure to vacuum away all dust from the test area so the duct tape will stick successfully.

TOOLS & MATERIALS

▪ Shop vac
▪ Aluminum foil
▪ Duct tape

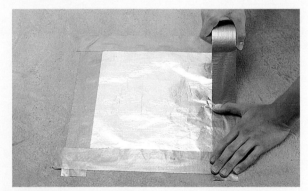

1 To conduct the dampness test, start by cleaning and drying a small section of the floor. Cover it with aluminum foil, and tape down the edges.

2 Wait one day. If the concrete under the patch is wet, the dampness must have risen through the floor because the foil stopped condensation from forming.

REPAIRING CONCRETE FLOORS

project

To get the best bond between the existing concrete and the patching material, slightly undercut the top edges of the crack. Hold a cold chisel against the concrete just below the crack opening. Tip it so it forms about a 45 degree angle to the surface, and strike it with a mason's hammer. Do this for the length of the crack on both sides. The goal is to provide something that the patch can grip that is below the surface of the concrete.

TOOLS & MATERIALS

▪ Masonry hammer and cold chisel
▪ Gloves
▪ Brush
▪ Mason's and concrete finishing trowels
▪ Cement patch

3 Use a mason's trowel to fill the crack with patching compound. Patching products are usually cement/acrylic formulations that are easy to use and durable. Quick-setting hydraulic cement (used to stop water leaks in masonry walls) works well in dry applications, too. It swells slightly as it sets to make a tight bond.

1 Use a cold chisel and a masonry hammer to chip away the rough edges of each crack. Use the same tools to deepen shallow sections to create more surface area for the patching material to grip. Be sure to wear heavy leather gloves while doing this job. These gloves can deflect hammer blows that slip off of the chisel.

2 Once the chiseling is done, brush all dust and debris from the crack. Use a shop vac to remove fine dust. Read and follow the site preparation instructions on the patching-material package. Usually, they recommend brushing water and a liquid bonding agent into the crack before applying the patching material.

4 Once the crack is filled with patching compound, apply extra patch across the top of the crack, and force it into the surface. Then spread it just like drywall joint compound is applied to a wall or ceiling. Use a finishing trowel (instead of a mason's trowel) for this because it is bigger and more flexible.

5 Feather the edges of the patch. As you work on the edge of the patch, where it meets the dry concrete floor, sprinkle a small amount of water on the patch to make the trowelled surface smoother. Spray water on the patch three or four times over the next two days to improve setting strength.

Tiling Floors

project

One of the best ways to maintain tile alignment is by snapping reference chalk lines on the subfloor. (See pages 40–41.) Even when these lines are covered with mastic, they can usually be seen through the notches in the mastic. You can snap a line for every course of tile. But good results are achieved with lines that repeat every 2 or 3 tiles. With good planning and using tile spacers, it's almost impossible to install the tiles incorrectly.

TOOLS & MATERIALS

▌ Chalk-line box ▌ Tile
▌ Notched trowel
▌ Tile adhesive
▌ Tile spacers
▌ Layout stick (optional)

1 Plan a tile layout on paper first; then snap chalk line guides on the floor, and set out a few rows of tile to spot any unexpected problems with the layout. Fitting the tiles before the mastic is applied gives you plenty of time to make changes without worrying about the open time of the mastic.

3 Start laying the tiles by lowering each into the mastic, using the chalk lines as a guide. Push each tile firmly into the mastic; then twist it slightly to make sure a good bond is achieved. If mastic gets on the surface of any tile, remove it before continuing. It's much harder to remove later.

4 Some tiles are manufactured with alignment ears, or nubs, on all four edges. These ears maintain uniform spacing (and thus uniform grout joints) between all of the tiles. Just push each tile tightly against the others. If your tiles don't have these ears, use tile spacers to maintain the correct spacing between tiles.

2 Once you are satisfied with the tile layout, remove the tile; sweep the floor clean; and start applying the tile mastic. The adhesive instructions will recommend a sensible working area based on the drying time of the adhesive. They will also stipulate the size of the notches on the trowel you use. Hold the trowel at a 45-deg. angle.

5 Another good way to keep tiles aligned, especially on large installations, is to use a layout stick made of 1x2 or 1x4 pine lumber. (See page 65.) When placed next to the installed tile, you'll know at a glance if the layout is uniform. Move misaligned tiles to match the marks.

LAYING OUT FLOORS

LASER LEVELS emit a light beam that shows clearly on almost any surface. The tools are used mainly to establish level points. But they are also handy in tile work, where they can project layout lines.

Battery-powered laser levels project a beam of light. You can use one to establish level points or to display working guidelines on floors and walls.

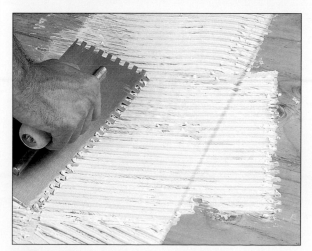

With a laser layout line projected across the floor, you don't have to hold back adhesive to keep from covering the line the way you must with chalk lines.

INSTALLING PARTIAL TILES

project

There are several ways to cut partial tiles. The most common choice is to buy an inexpensive tile snap cutter (for straight cuts) and some tile nippers (to make curved cuts). These tools work well, and because you own them, you can use them whenever you want. The better approach to cutting tiles, however, is with an electric wet saw specifically designed for the job. These rental items are a little smaller than a power miter saw and make very clean cuts.

TOOLS & MATERIALS
- Tile ▪ Marker or pencil
- Snap tile cutter and finishing stone
- Scoring tool ▪ Tile nippers
- Notched trowel, tile adhesive, and spacers

1 The easiest way to mark a border tile that needs to be cut is to do the job with the tile in place. First, place the border tile directly over the last full tile on the floor. Then place another full tile on top of the border tile, and push this tile against the wall. Use the back edge of top tile as a guide for marking the border tile.

4 Once the glaze is cut, return the scoring handle to the fence at the front edge of the tile, and press down firmly. The plate on the scoring arm presses down equally on both sides of the cut and snaps the tile in two. Smooth rough edges using an inexpensive hand finishing stone that's available at tile stores and home centers.

5 Spread mastic on the floor using a notched trowel. Then press the tile into the mastic, and twist it slightly to make a good bond. Slide tile spacers into place to keep the grout joints uniform. Wipe up any mastic that may be on the surface, and cut and install the next border tile.

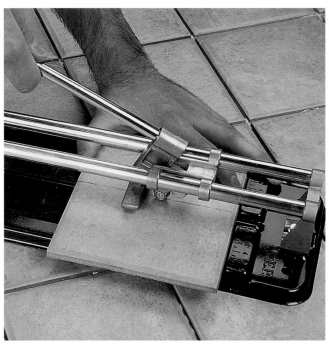

2 Once the tile is marked, place it in a snap tile cutter and push it against the fence. Score the tile along the cut line by pulling the scoring arm toward you. Use firm, even pressure. One scoring pass should be all that's required to cut through the glaze and make it possible to snap the tile with the tool.

3 The scoring wheel on a snap cutter is made of very hard steel and is designed to break through the glaze on top of ceramic tile but not to cut though the tile. Once the glaze is broken, it's an easy matter to snap the tile in two pieces. For best results, make sure the wheel and cut line are aligned exactly before pulling the wheel.

6 Cutting around obstructions is a part of nearly every tile job. The best approach is to mark the tile in place, then use a scoring tool to cut through the glaze along the cut line (inset). Once the glaze is scored, use tile nippers to cut away the waste. Remove small pieces instead of large ones, working to the cut line gradually.

7 Use a coarse file, or a wood dowel wrapped in coarse sandpaper, to smooth the cut made with the tile nippers. Then test fit the tile next to the obstruction. Once you are satisfied with the fit, spread adhesive on the floor; then install the tile. Make sure to maintain proper grout spacing around all edges.

Tiling Floors

project

Removing extra grout after all the joints are filled is not a difficult job, but it can be annoying. Clean the tile using plenty of clean water. Each time you wipe the floor with a sponge, rinse it in water. As soon as the water in your bucket starts to get cloudy, replace it with clean water. No matter how careful you are, a fine haze will almost always be left behind when the surface dries. Just buff this away with a clean cloth to finish the job.

TOOLS & MATERIALS

- Bucket, sponges, and water
- Rags
- Grout mix and stirring tool
- Grout float
- Silicone grout sealer

1 There are two basic types of tile grout: dry powder that needs to be mixed with water, and premixed that is used directly from the container. Dry grout can be colored with pigment to achieve a different look than standard white. Mix up only the amount you can comfortably apply at one time.

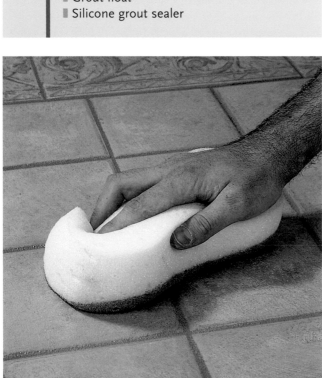

3 As the grout starts to set, smooth the joints with your finger or the end of a wood dowel. Then clean up the excess grout using a damp sponge. Wipe in all directions, and rinse the sponge in clean water frequently. Don't use a wet sponge because extra water weakens the bond between the grout and the tile.

4 Grout can also be removed from the surface using a damp rag. A rag does, however, tend to pull grout out of the joints more than a sponge because it does not have as uniform a surface. Rags are best used to remove haze at the final stages of the job. A slightly damp (or even dry) rag can do the job without harming the grout.

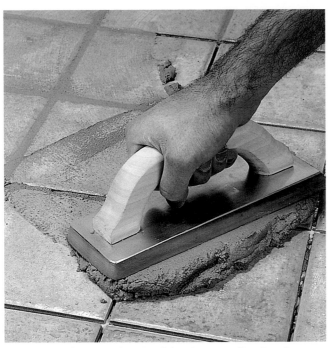

2 Once the grout is mixed, begin spreading it using a rubber-faced grout float. Work with long strokes, in a diagonal direction to the grid of the tile. Apply firm pressure so that the grout is forced to the bottom of all the joints. Clean any extra grout from the surface with the edge of the float as you go. This can reduce cleanup time later.

5 In wet or damp areas, like kitchens and bathrooms, it's a good idea to seal the grout once it's cured. Typical liquid silicone sealers come in tubes with applicators designed to fit standard grout joints. To use the sealer, just squeeze the container slightly, and drag the tip over all of the joints.

THRESHOLDS

THRESHOLDS (sometimes called saddles) can be wood, metal, or marble strips that bridge gaps between different types of floors. They can also make a transition between floors that are almost but not quite level with each other—for example, where a tiled bath floor is slightly higher than the wood floor in a hallway. You attach the threshold to the underlayment and tile up to it. Most wood and metal saddles are attached with nails or screws. (You can conceal the screwheads in wooden saddles with putty or plugs.) Marble saddles, which are typically used at bathroom doors, are set in a bed of adhesive. Whatever type you use, plan for thresholds during the layout stage.

WOODEN THRESHOLD

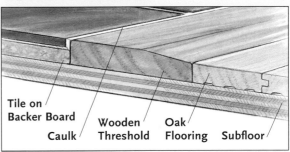

Tile on Backer Board
Caulk
Wooden Threshold
Oak Flooring
Subfloor

METAL THRESHOLD

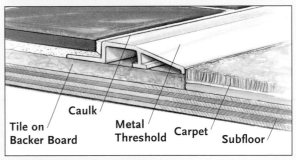

Caulk
Tile on Backer Board
Metal Threshold
Carpet
Subfloor

MARBLE THRESHOLD

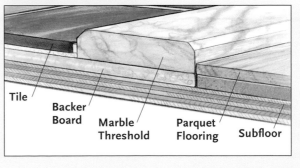

Tile
Backer Board
Marble Threshold
Parquet Flooring
Subfloor

PREPARING THE FLOOR FOR SLATE TILE

project

The easiest way to find loose spots in a subfloor is to walk slowly over the entire floor and listen for squeaks. If you hear anything, screw this area of the subfloor to the floor joists below. The best approach is to screw the entire subfloor to the joists. You may do some extra work this way. But it doesn't take long; it doesn't cost much; and it leads to a better job. Make sure that the heads of any screws that you do drive are recessed slightly.

TOOLS & MATERIALS

▌Hammer ▌Prybar ▌Locking pliers
▌Handsaw ▌Utility knife ▌¼-in.-thick backer board underlayment ▌Backer board nails or screws ▌Patching compound
▌6-in.-wide putty knife ▌Sandpaper
▌Slate floor tiles

1 Begin site preparation by removing all the baseboard and shoe moldings. Use a prybar and hammer, and work carefully to avoid damaging the wall. It's best to pry only in the areas above the studs. Use a stud finder, or look for nailhead depressions in the moldings, which will fall over the studs.

4 Make the cut with a crosscut handsaw. Carefully start the cut without damaging the casing. Then continue the cut and stop just before the board is cut through, finishing up with a sharp utility knife. This prevents damage from the saw that often occurs at the end of such a close-quarters cut.

5 Cover the floor with ¼-in.-thick cement backer boards. Cut these panels much like you cut drywall. Just score the surface with a utility knife, and snap the board apart. Use corrosion-resistant nails (or screws) made for this material to install it. Work in a 4- to 5-in.-sq. pattern, and recess the heads below the surface.

2 Once a piece of molding is pried off of the wall, remove the nails by pulling them out from the backside using locking pliers and a scrap block. By doing this, the outside surface of the board is not harmed, and it can be reused, after the floor tiles have been installed.

3 When you install a new floor, the floor height is raised and the tile won't fit under the door casing boards. These boards must be cut so that the new flooring will fit. To mark for these cuts, place a piece of underlayment and a new tile on top of the floor, and scribe the casing along the top of this tile.

6 Once all the underlayment is installed, cover the nailheads (or screwheads) and the panel seams with floor-patching compound. Use a 6-in.-wide putty knife for this job, and spread the compound in the same way you apply drywall joint compound. Feather the compound so that it's smooth with the surrounding surface.

7 After the compound dries, sand away any rough sections. Then place the slate on the floor to check for the best layout. If you are using tiles that vary in color like these, place the most attractive ones in the most visible spots. Also, try to maintain even spacing around the borders to keep border tiles the same size.

INSTALLING THE SLATE

Taking the time and trouble to dry lay slate tiles before installing them makes good sense. These natural stone products always vary in color and texture, sometimes dramatically. So the only way to get a clear picture of how the finished job will look is to spread them out and tinker with the arrangement. Attractive slates should be placed in the most visible areas, while less appealing tiles should go along walls, behind doors, or underneath furniture.

TOOLS & MATERIALS

▮ Circular saw with an abrasive blade
▮ Wood or plastic grout spacers ▮ Notched trowel ▮ Flat pointing trowel ▮ Mastic
▮ Grout and grout sealer ▮ Sponge
▮ Burlap bag ▮ Sawdust ▮ Paintbrush

1 Slate tiles are easy to cut using a circular saw and an abrasive or masonry blade. Making these cuts is almost as fast as cutting through wood. But it creates a lot more noise and dust, and can even send small shards of stone flying. Because of this, wear eye, ear, and breathing protection when cutting slate.

4 When all the tiles are laid, allow the floor to dry according to the mastic-maker's directions. When the mastic has set, mix up some grout and spread a wide bead (approximately ½- to ¾-in. diameter) over all the joints. Force the grout into the joints with a flat pointing trowel. This tool is easy to use.

5 Clean up the grout before it dries because it's much harder to do later. The best tools for this job are a large sponge and a big bucket of clean water. The sponge should be damp, not wet, because excess water will weaken the grout. Rinse the sponge frequently, and when the bucket water gets cloudy, replace it.

2 Plan the job so that you end up in a doorway so you can get out of the area without walking on the freshly laid tile. Apply the mastic in small sections so it doesn't start to dry before it can be covered with tile. Hold the notched trowel at a 45-deg. angle.

3 Carefully place each tile in the mastic, and twist it back-and-forth slightly to make sure it is covered with mastic. Then press it firmly into its finished position. Use tile spacers to keep the grout lines consistent, and wipe any mastic that may be on the surface of the tile with a damp rag.

6 After the grout has cured, there will be a haze on the surface of the tile. On smooth tiles, this can be removed by buffing the surface with a clean, dry cloth. But on rough textured tile, like these slate tiles, rubbing the surface with sawdust works better. Just spread some on the floor, and rub it in a circular motion using a burlap rag.

7 Finish up the job by sealing the tile and grout with a liquid sealer. Just brush it on according to the package directions, and make sure it penetrates all the grout joints. Many sealers recommend waiting for several weeks after the installation is complete before applying the sealer.

design ideas

Mosaic tiles, above left, add texture to a bathroom floor.

Kitchen floors, above, were made for ceramic and stone tiles.

Stone tiles, left, are a good choice for mudrooms and entries.

Traditional designs, below, are possible with mosaic tiles.

Natural stone, opposite, sets the stage for a dramatic inset design.

Tiling Floors

Hexagon tiles, below, provide a transition to outside.

Marble, right, adds an elegant touch.

Tile inset, below right, creates a dramatic entry.

Terra-cotta tiles, opposite, work well in mudrooms.

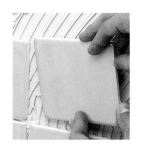

tiling walls

4

BECAUSE TILES RESIST heat, water, and a variety of stains, they are well suited to adorn walls, especially kitchen and bathroom walls where easy maintenance is a prime concern. In kitchens, of course, tiles often bridge the gap between countertops and upper cabinets. In bathrooms, tile is often used to line shower stalls and tub surrounds. But you can give a bathroom a more open, unified feeling by extending the tile to adjacent walls. Behind a vanity, you can extend a tile backsplash up the wall to frame a mirror. And wall tiles with trim strips can frame windows, doors, and other architectural features in any room of the house.

Tiling Walls

LAYOUT AND PREPARATION

The same basic design considerations that apply to tiling floors—color, size, shape, texture, and pattern—also apply to walls. However, when planning your layout, bear in mind that most wall applications incorporate a design that uses tiles of contrasting colors. This makes estimating the number of tiles a bit more difficult and requires a more precise layout.

Tile work on walls often involves different types and shapes of trim pieces, such as tiles with a bullnose edge. You may also need to use special shapes to handle inside and outside corners. These special shapes can make a tile job look very elegant, but they complicate the layout. You need to account for the grout joints, of course, but also for the odd-size portion of the trim piece that turns an inside or outside corner.

If you plan to tile both the walls and the floor, you have two sets of layouts to deal with. Each one may require an adjustment to make a balanced installation. But you need to concentrate on the area along the floor where the two systems meet. You should align grout seams there if at all possible.

One approach is to start these projects by installing the row of cove or other finishing tiles at the floor level. Coves make a very low-maintenance detail (a great help in kitchens and baths) because the rounded cove base eliminates hard-edged, dirt-trapping corners.

Because this row makes the transition between floor and wall, it's important to have full tiles on both sides if possible. That means you can't adjust the main tile field of the floor on one side, or the wall on the other, which could leave small, partial tiles at the opposite wall or the ceiling. The best bet is to lay out tiles with spacers for grout joints (or make an accurate layout stick) and see where the field tiles will fall.

Once you have positioned the cove tiles, you can work your way up the wall. Save the floor for last so that you don't damage or blemish the new tile with adhesive or grout as you work on the wall.

Patterns and Unique Designs

Many tile manufacturers now make integrated tile systems. For example, in addition to field tiles they offer rectangular pieces for borders, half-rounded accent strips, caps, and several other shapes all designed to work in the same basic grid. With these systems it is relatively easy to plan out a repeating wall scheme.

DESIGN OPTIONS

NO DESIGN IS BAD if it's in your own house and represents the style you like. Colors and patterns are matters of personal taste, after all. But before you undertake a tile project covering most or all of a wall, it pays to experiment.

You can do this on a piece of graph paper, using colored pencils to sketch in your ideas at a realistic scale. You may be able to use home-design software to create tile patterns complete with bath fixtures, lights, and a mirror.

Now some home-center chains and design-build contracting firms also offer computer-aided design (CAD) services. They allow you to plan a layout and try different combinations of tile. The most sophisticated software creates three-dimensional views showing how the finished project might look.

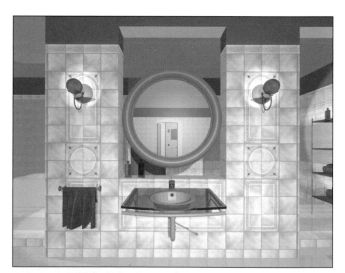

Computer-aided design software programs let you experiment with different tile patterns and colors on your home computer screen.

If you are creating your own design, the amount of detail you can include is determined in part by three elements: the size of the wall, the size of the design, and the size of the tiles. Bear in mind that geometric patterns are the easiest to create and install because the basic building blocks are geometric units. It's more difficult to create and install a free-flowing pattern. For example, if you want to create a curved design along a set of stairs, you will have to make many precise cuts.

Cutting Tiles

Cut tiles should be more than half a tile wide. Ideally, they should be equal widths at opposite sides of a room, to provide symmetry. Sometimes you can adjust the edge sizes by adjusting the width of all the grout joints.

Also be aware of where cut tiles may be needed around doorways, windows, cabinets, and countertops, and whether it would look better to plan the layout so that partial tiles are moved away from these focal points. For example, cut tiles on either side of a window or door opening should be the same width for the opening to appear centered. In the same way, if you are tiling around a fireplace, the wall installation will probably look best if you use full tiles on the sides and save partial tiles or irregular pieces for the corners of the room.

Accent tiles help break up a field of same-color tiles such as shown on this countertop and backsplash.

With computer design programs, you can create a rough view of an area using stock versions of rugs and other fixtures to build your "before" picture.

Define the area you want to change, the floor in this case, and insert different shapes and patterns that change carpeting into tile.

Tiling Walls

Planning for Materials

To estimate the amount of tiles you need, disregard small obstructions when you're measuring square footage. Subtract only for a large window, built-in sink, or cabinet. It's wise to figure about 5 to 10 percent for waste. If your installation includes different-color tiles, use your drawing to count the actual number of tiles of each color, adding the same percentage for miscuts and breakage. If the layout includes cut tiles, count each partial tile as a full tile.

If you are extending tile to adjoining walls or across a doorway, you will want to align the horizontal grout joints. It's often best to use full tiles where walls join, but you should check how the field tiles will fall when they reach the edges of the project area. If you center full tiles over a doorway, for example, you might end up with cut tiles of two different widths at opposite ends of the wall. You can't very well reshape your rooms to match a tile grid. But if you check several possible layouts, you can generally find one that has full tiles where you notice the pattern and partial tiles where you don't.

If you're working with mural tiles (or almost any distinct pattern within the main tile field), you may need to account for a large block of tiles. Most murals come in sets of tiles—from as few as four to well over 50—with each tile representing a piece of the picture. Plan these installations by taking the overall dimensions of the mural and making adjustments. You may be able to avoid small pieces at the corners by using border tiles.

BASIC TILE COMBINATIONS

YOU CAN USE DIFFERENT SIZES, SHAPES, AND COLORS to create a nearly limitless number of tile patterns and combinations. But even if you stick to one size, there are three basic ways to set them on the wall.

Jack-on-Jack. This is the easiest way to lay wall tiles, stacking one tile directly on top of another.

Running Bond. This is the same kind of pattern used on most brick walls, with the joints of one course centered under full tiles in the next row.

Diagonal Jack-on-Jack. This is the basic system of aligned joints turned sideways 45 degrees. The drawback is that every tile in the rows at the floor and ceiling has to be trimmed.

Jack-on-jack layouts have tiles stacked directly on top of each other in columns. With this system, all the grout joints between tiles are aligned.

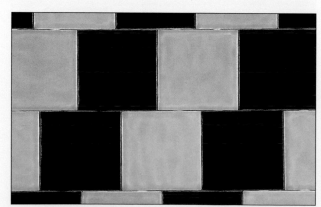

Running bond layouts have the joints in one course offset to fall over the center of tiles below. The offset is accentuated with contrasting colors.

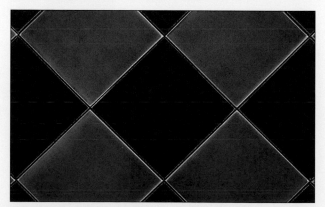

Diagonal jack-on-jack layouts have the basic stacked tile pattern turned sideways on the wall. This gives square tiles a diamond-shaped appearance.

EXTENDING AN ELECTRICAL BOX

project

The surface requirements for a wall that's going to be tiled aren't very involved. One thing that may not come to mind is adding extensions to the boxes that hold receptacles, switches, and even wall-mounted lights. Electrical boxes must be installed so that they are flush with the finished surface. After you add backer board and tile to a wall, it may increase by ½ in. or more, which leaves the electrical boxes recessed too far into the wall. Adding box extensions fixes this problem.

TOOLS & MATERIALS

- Box extender
- Screwdriver
- Backer board
- Backer-board screws

1 First determine the thickness of the backer board you are going to install for the tile. Then turn off the power to any circuits that service the work area, and check for power with a current tester at each receptacle, switch, and light fixture. Then remove the electrical cover plates, and unscrew the electrical devices.

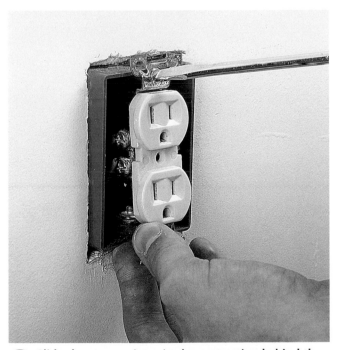

2 Slide the appropriate size box extension behind the receptacle or switch, and screw it to the existing box. Code-approved extensions are a common home center item. But if you can't find them in your local store, go to an electrical supply outlet where you'll be sure to find them.

3 Cut the backer board to fit tightly around the box extension, and screw these panels to the wall with backer-board screws. Then install the tile; grout the joints; and clean the surface. Once the job is complete, tighten the screws that hold the receptacle or switch to the box; then add the cover plate.

Tiling Walls

REMOVING A BASE TRIM

Interior trim work can be difficult and expensive to install. If you have attractive trim on any wall that you plan to cover with tile, it makes sense to remove the trim carefully so that you can replace it after the tile is installed, or use it elsewhere in the house. The keys are to work slowly and gently. Also, protect the wall, floor, and other trim boards with cedar shingles when you are working with a pry bar. For best results use several different size pry bars to fit different situations.

TOOLS & MATERIALS

- Pry bars ▪ Screwdriver ▪ Hammer
- Cedar shimming shingles
- Masking tape and marker

1 The basic clamshell baseboard is a one-piece affair that is made of pine and is easy to remove. But multiple-piece baseboard assemblies, like this, require more effort and care. The first step is to remove the shoe molding along the floor. Then pry off the base cap from the top of the main baseboard and set it aside.

3 On long sections of baseboard, you'll need several pry bars, flat blade screwdrivers, chisels, tapered shingles, wood wedges, and other prying implements. Start at one end, and work progressively to the other. Once the board is free, you can pull the nails out from the back side of the board.

4 For sections of baseboard that you can't remove, pry the board off the wall as much as possible. Then place a bar between the baseboard and the wall, next to the nails. Hold a shingle on the surface, and tap the baseboard. This should expose the nailheads; pull them out using a nail puller.

2 Unlike the shoe and base cap moldings, the main baseboard is usually attached with at least two nails per stud. Because of this, it's more difficult to remove. To do the job, locate the studs in the wall; place a cedar shimming shingle over each stud location; and push a pry bar between the shingle and the back of the baseboard.

5 Label the back of each piece you remove using masking tape and a felt marker. If you are dealing with only a couple of boards, this isn't necessary. But if you have a roomful of trim boards, it will be much easier and faster to reinstall them later if they are marked.

PREPARING WALLS FOR TILE

MOST INTERIOR WALLS are surfaced with gypsum wallboard. In many older homes the walls are plastered. Both materials generally make a good backing for ceramic tile if the surface is sound, flat, and smooth. You can also tile over wood or masonry walls. It's not a good idea to tile over wallpaper, fabric, or any other surface that is not strong enough, by itself, to support tile. These should be removed before applying tile.

In new construction, of course, a taped and finished drywall surface will make an ideal base for tile. But in existing rooms, you may have to make some repairs and improvements to make sure the tile job will last. There are two basic options: bury surface problems under a new layer of drywall, or fix the existing wall.

In addition to the surface repairs, you may want to make some changes that are more than skin deep, such as relocating an electrical outlet or moving an in-wall air conditioner. Fix any problems that affect the framing.

Existing Surfaces. A wall is considered too weak for tile if you can flex the surface by pressing the heel of your hand against a panel midway between two studs. Adding another layer of drywall should do the trick, but you will need to compensate for the added thickness around windows and doors.

Even if the wallboard or plaster is sound, you should not set tile if the surface paint is loose or peeling. Prepare these surfaces basically the same way you would for repainting—by scraping away any loose paint, filling the gouges with joint compound, and roughing up glossy surfaces with sandpaper.

Walls in Wet Areas. If you are tiling a wall that's subject to moisture or water, you need to install some type of waterproofing membrane, water-resistant backing, or both. The most common solution is a layer of cement-based backer board attached with corrosion-resistant nails or screws. Depending on the extent of the moisture exposure, a waterproof membrane also may be required. You should check local building codes for recommended waterproofing methods in your area.

Tiling Walls

Patching Drywall

The good news is that you don't have to patch every minor dent and scratch, because they will be filled by the tile adhesive. But you should repair holes and fix popped nails, bubbled joint tape, and other problems that could keep the tile from sitting flat on the wall.

Instead of driving loose nails back into drywall, pull them and drive a drywall screw near the old hole. Along joints, check for splits or bubbles in the drywall tape. If you find raised or loose sections, slice the damaged tape from the wall using a utility knife, and replace it with fiberglass mesh tape embedded in the tile adhesive.

There are several ways to repair larger cracks and holes. The most drastic is to cut out a section of the damaged drywall running from one stud to another, although this entails so much cutting that you might as well replace the entire sheet. In most cases, you can add mesh to reinforce a patch or cut out the damaged area and add a patch piece of solid drywall.

Over small holes—for example, where you have some crumbling around holes for plumbing pipes—you can use self-stick fiberglass mesh to bridge the gaps and reinforce a filling layer of joint compound. For doorknob-sized holes, you can use a mesh patch kit that comes with an extra reinforcing panel.

One good way to fix large holes is to cut a clean-edged rectangular opening around the damage, and reinforce the edges with short lengths of 1x3 fastened to the inside face of the drywall. The exposed edges of the wood strips can support a solid drywall patch.

PATCHING SMALL HOLES

When you're making a repair, don't try to save sections or edges of drywall that seem weak. Cut back until you reach solid material that will support the new tile.

TOOLS & MATERIALS

■ Drywall taping knife ■ Fiberglass mesh tape ■ Mesh patch kit ■ Joint compound

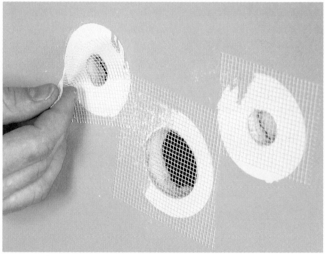

1 Bridge small holes and gaps with self-stick fiberglass mesh tape. It keeps patch material from falling through the hole and reinforces the repair.

2 Joint compound will embed in the mesh. You will probably need one coat to fill the hole and another to smooth over the surface.

3 Over larger holes, you can use a self-stick patch kit. Peel off the backing; install the reinforcing panel face down; and finish the mesh surface.

PATCHING LARGE HOLES

Use dry furring strips or other wood strips to avoid shrinking that could disrupt the patch repair and the tiles above.

TOOLS & MATERIALS

▌ Drywall saw or utility knife ▌ 1x3s
▌ Caulking gun and adhesive ▌ Drill and drywall screws ▌ Drywall taping knife
▌ Tape and joint compound ▌ Sandpaper, sanding pad, or sanding mesh

1 Cut out the damaged area, leaving a clean-edged rectangle. Then cut 1x3 furring strips; hold them to the drywall; and fasten with screws.

2 Apply construction adhesive to the exposed half of the side braces. You can also add adhesive to the furring strips before you install them.

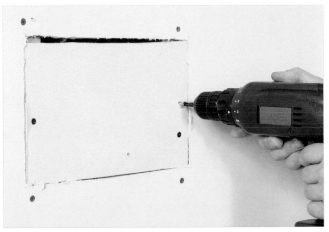

3 Set the patch piece of drywall on the braces; move it back and forth to set in the adhesive; and secure it with drywall screws.

4 Make sure that the screwheads are flush, and cover the seams with paper or fiberglass tape embedded in joint compound.

5 With tile, you don't need to make a perfect repair, but you may want to add one extra coat, and sand away rough edges of compound.

Tiling Walls

PATCHING PLASTER

It's wise to seal large areas of fresh plaster or joint compound so that the dry material does not pull excessive moisture from the tile adhesive and weaken the tile bond.

TOOLS & MATERIALS

- Wide drywall taping knife
- Patching plaster ▮ Primer and roller or brush ▮ Masonry trowel

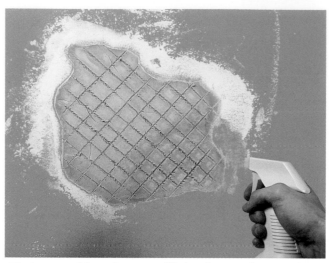

1 Use patching plaster to fill the damaged area in layers. Score the undercoat surface. When dry, moisten before troweling on the finish coat.

2 Use a wide blade to smooth out the finish coat. Let one edge ride on the adjacent wall to keep the patch flush. Sand down any ridges.

3 When the finish coat is dry, prime the patch to keep the dry, unsealed material from drawing moisture from the tile adhesive.

Preparing and Repairing Plaster

Extensive cracking in a plaster wall often indicates regular seasonal movement in the building, which can disrupt tile. In severe cases, you may need to strip the surface, although a layer of glued-and-screwed cement backer board may work. If the plaster is soft and cracks or crumbles when you poke it with a screwdriver, it should be removed.

Fill small holes or depressions with patching plaster. Clean and moisten the area, and spread the fresh plaster with a wide drywall taping knife. When the patch dries, fill it to the surface; let it dry; and sand it flush.

If the plaster is sound, wash it thoroughly with a general-purpose cleaner to remove dirt or grease. Sand a glossy painted surface to ensure a good adhesive bond.

Repairing Outside Corners

Corners that project into a room (around pass-through openings, for example) often take the most abuse and show the most damage—both in drywall and plaster walls. If the damage is minor, you can usually repair it with drywall joint compound and a wide drywall knife. Use a straightedge to shape the corner edge, or smooth out one side and let it dry before you work on the adjoining surface.

If the damage is extensive, you may need to cut away the corner reinforcement. Although some corners may have only paper-taped edges that are easy to remove, most have metal corner guards secured with nails. Once the guard is damaged, you may have to pull the nails and remove it (or a piece of it) and install new edging.

FIXING A CORNER

If the corner guard has a dent in it but is still secure, try filling the area with joint compound. Always replace a loose guard.

TOOLS & MATERIALS

▪ Utility knife ▪ Hacksaw ▪ Metal snips
▪ Corner guard ▪ Drill and screws
▪ Putty knife and joint compound

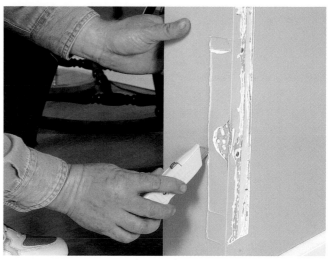

1 To get at a damaged section of corner guard, you may have to cut through layers of paint and joint compound with a utility knife.

2 Once the guard is exposed, use a hacksaw to cut through the metal above and below the damaged section. Pull the nails, and remove it.

3 Use metal snips to cut a replacement length of guard. Clear away loose drywall paper and compound on the corner before you fasten the piece.

4 Use drywall screws to fasten the replacement guard on the corner. Make sure that the raised corner rib aligns with the original guard.

5 Provide a flat surface for the tile by filling in both sides of the raised corner rib with joint compound. Sand off any raised ridges.

Tiling Walls

INSTALLING DRYWALL

project

Most people use drywall (gypsum wallboard) to cover new and old walls alike. It's inexpensive, relatively easy to install, and when finished properly, provides a smooth, flawless surface for a final finish, such as tile. For new construction, most people choose ½-in.-thick panels as the default. If you are covering an existing wall, you can use the thinner ⅜-in.-thick panels.

TOOLS & MATERIALS

▌Measuring tape and marker ▌Utility knife ▌Drywall saw ▌Drywall panel lifter ▌Drill with a screwdriver bits and screws ▌Drywall finishing tape ▌Drywall joint compound ▌Taping knives and compound pan

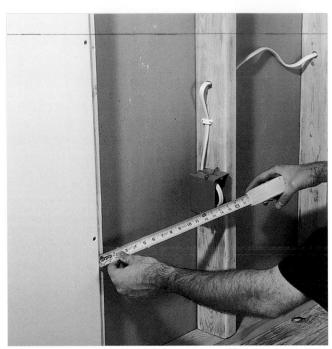

1 Use a measuring tape to locate electrical outlets and other obstructions. Because there may be a gap between the bottom panel and the floor, which will be covered with baseboard trim, measure from the ceiling down to the top of the box, and then measure horizontally from the edge of the last sheet to the side of the box.

4 To cut a panel to width, measure for the cut, and then snap a chalk line. Cut along this line using a utility knife. You don't have to cut through the panel, just cut through the paper that covers the gypsum core.

5 Once the panel is scored, move it so that the cut line falls just past the edge of your worktable. Hold down the main panel with one hand; then snap down the waste side of the panel with your other hand. To finish the cut, run a sharp utility knife through the paper on the backside of the panel.

2 Transfer the measurements to the front of a drywall sheet; add the electrical box dimensions; and draw the four lines that form the box. Before making any cuts, check the measurements from the ceiling, the floor, and the last sheet that was installed.

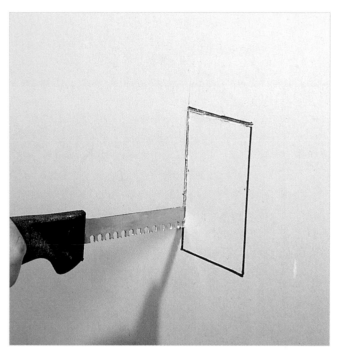

3 Use a drywall saw to make the cuts. This tool has a sharp point on the end so that you can push it in anywhere along the lines and start cutting. Another option is a drywall cutout tool that looks like a small router. You can use this tool to cut the opening in a down position or after the sheet is partially attached to the wall.`

6 Lean the cut panel against the wall, and slide a panel lifter under the bottom edge. This simple device is slightly bow-shaped so when you step on the outside end, the inside end moves up and lifts the panel with it. When the panel is tight against the ceiling, attach it with screws (inset).

7 To finish drywall for tile, just cover the screw- or nailheads with joint compound; then cover the seams with paper tape and a single coat of compound. The second and third coats of compound, which are typical on finished drywall, aren't necessary unless tile will cover only part of the wall.

Tiling Walls

PLANNING THE TILE LAYOUT

project

As with many projects, proper planning is one of the most important steps in any wall-tiling job. But making sure that the walls are strong and stable is only part of the prep job. You must lay out the walls carefully so that the tile will fit properly. This means marking a series of tile guidelines on the wall. For simple installations, establish a horizontal working line near the base of the wall and a vertical line near the center of the wall.

TOOLS & MATERIALS
▌ Layout stick and marker
▌ Level
▌ Chalk-line box
▌ Measuring tape

1 On most walls, the horizontal layout is the most important because the bottom row of tiles is usually highly visible. As a general rule of thumb, plan for the bottom tiles to be no smaller than half a tile. Once the horizontal starting point is established, use a layout stick to transfer the tile and grout lines up the wall.

4 Once the main horizontal layout is drawn, use a layout stick to mark the tile joint lines at both ends of the wall. Connect these with a chalk line. To achieve the most accurate line, pin the middle of the string against the wall with one hand; then snap one side of the string, followed by the other side.

5 Use a layout stick to mark the location of the tiles along the snapped line; then choose a vertical layout line using a level. You may have to accept a row of small tiles in one area to end up with good spacing around a countertop and a row of wall cabinets or some other more visible area.

2 After the course lines have been marked, hold a full tile against the layout stick to double check the size of the top tile. The bigger this tile is, the better the job will look. Plan for one that is at least one-half the size of a full tile. If you must use smaller tiles, try to locate them in out-of-view places like under wall cabinets.

3 Choose a convenient tile mark near the middle of the wall and extend this mark from side to side using a long level. Be careful when making this line because it provides the basis for the square alignment of all the tiles on the wall. On very long walls, place the level on a long straight 2x4 to minimize the chance of mistakes.

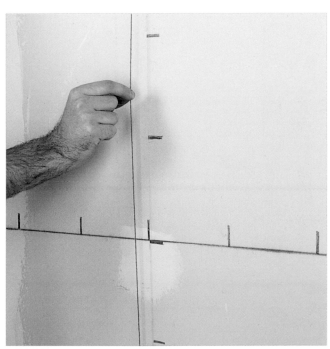

6 Indicate the main vertical guide by snapping a chalk line. To make a series of vertical layout lines, draw a line along the bottom of the wall with a layout stick and do the same along the top of the wall. Then snap chalk lines between the layout marks. Also draw lines or snap chalk lines to indicate the position of obstructions.

7 Take the time to note the location of structural elements behind the wallboard. These could be difficult to find after the tile is installed. The built-in framing for such things as grab bars and toilet paper holders are good examples. You can write them on paper, but using the floor makes sure you'll never lose the dimensions.

Tiling Walls

INSTALLING AND FINISHING TILES

Tiles are not difficult to install, but it takes more time to do this job than it seems at first. Part of the problem is that you are always working against a deadline, which is the open time of the adhesive you use. If it starts to set before you get the tiles installed, the bond is weakened and this undermines the whole job. Open time is usually listed on the adhesive container. If it isn't, plan on working on an area that's no bigger than 4 feet square.

TOOLS & MATERIALS

- Level ▪ Hammer and nails
- Measuring tape ▪ Notched trowel and adhesive ▪ Tiles and spacers ▪ Grout
- Grout float and sponge

1 Establish the baseline for the wall tiles with a level and a pencil. Keep in mind that some tile jobs will be finished at the floor with some type of base trim—either trim tiles or a wood-base assembly. In both cases, the space underneath the baseline should be wide enough to accommodate the trim.

4 Set each wall tile into the adhesive, and twist it slightly so that it seats completely. If the tiles have alignment ears built into their edges, the grout joints between tiles should be consistent. If not, use small tile spacers to maintain alignment. Just slide the spacer between the tiles (inset), and press them against the wall.

5 One way to finish the bottom of a wall is to use full-size tiles. After the adhesive under the field tiles cures, remove the nails, and spread adhesive on the bottom of the wall. Press the bottom tile into the adhesive, and apply small pieces of tape to keep them from slipping down as the adhesive dries.

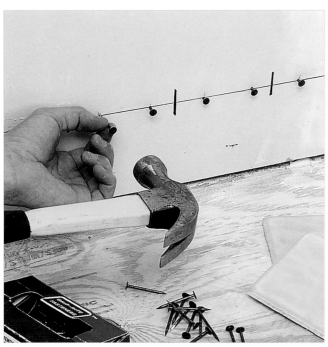

2 Lay out the tile spacing along the baseline using a layout stick. Then drive two nails between each grout joint to support the wall tile that will fall above the line. Drywall nails are the best choice for this job. Make sure the heads are at least ½ inch from the surface of the wall. Do this along the full length of the wall.

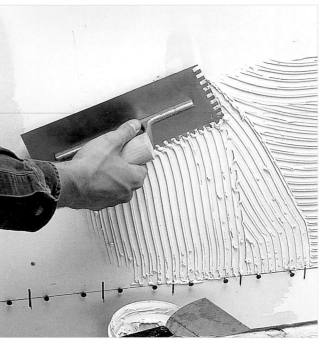

3 Once all the support nails are driven, mix a batch of adhesive, and start spreading it on the wall using a notched trowel. The adhesive package will stipulate the proper notch size, the trowel angle for the best coverage, and the working (or open) time of the adhesive. These guidelines vary depending on the manufacturer.

6 When all the tiles are installed and the adhesive is cured properly, apply grout to the surface. Spread the grout on the wall using a rubber-faced grout float. Work with sweeping diagonal strokes, and press the grout firmly into the joints. Remove the excess grout with the float as you work across the wall.

7 As the grouts sets, clean the surface of the tile with a damp (but not wet) sponge. Too much water can weaken the bond between the grout and the tile. Rinse the sponge in clean water frequently as you work. Let everything dry. Then remove the fine haze that usually forms by buffing the surface with a clean, dry rag.

Tiling Walls

Tile complements just about any design theme, below. Note how this tile works well with the marble tub surround and the dark wood.

Use tile, right, to create a decorative nook that can double as a shelf for often-used items.

Mosaic tiles, right bottom, make an attractive and functional backdrop on this half wall.

A geometric pattern of glass mosaic tiles, opposite, contributes to the sophisticated design of this kitchen.

Tiling Walls

Tiling Walls

design ideas

Glass tiles, opposite top left, complement contemporary cabinets.

Mosaic tiles, opposite top right, support a focal-point window.

Stone tiles, opposite bottom, add an elegant touch to a mudroom wall.

Random colors, left, add interest to a tile backsplash.

A step pattern, below left, adds drama behind a range.

Border tiles, below right, contain a colorful field of tiles.

design ideas

Decorative accents, right, add sparkle to a subtle design.

Natural stone, below, grounds a room filled with light.

Metal tiles, opposite top left, complement a modern design scheme.

Tumbled marble, opposite bottom left, creates a classical feeling in this bathroom.

Mosaic tiles, opposite right, extend from the wall into the shower.

tiling countertops 5

A CERAMIC OR STONE TILE COUNTER requires a proper base in order to last. You can adhere tile directly to plywood in dry locations, such as a display counter or tabletop, but for most kitchen and bathroom countertops, you will need either two layers of ¾-inch-thick plywood or a layer of plywood topped with a layer of tile backer board. The plywood-backerboard combination is the preferred method of installation around sinks and drainboards. If you skimp on these steps, your tile counter may crack, or the tiles may delaminate because the base of the counter is not rigid enough for the installation.

PLANNING THE LAYOUT

You can buy tile to meet the needs of a specific counter, or modify a new counter (or a replacement over existing cabinets) to fit your new tile. Modifying the counter is a good approach because it's easy to trim an extra inch or so off a sheet of plywood and backer board. And by deciding on your layout ahead of time, you may be able to create a counter of full tile and edging pieces.

To see how different edging styles will work, the best approach in the confined area of a countertop is to do a dry layout, using spacers to allow for grout seams. Here are some of the design issues to consider.

Overhangs. Be sure that the edge treatment provides enough clearance for top drawers in the cabinets and for undercounter appliances. If you run into clearance problems, choose edging tile with a narrow lip.

Bracing. Counters with large overhangs, such as serving counters or bars, may require some type of bracing to support the overhang. Even with combined layers of plywood and backer board, you should add braces where needed to make the countertop rigid.

Sink Installations. There are several types of sink mounts, including undercounter installation. But the most common type (and the one best suited to do-it-yourself projects) is a self-rimming sink. It has a lip that lies on top of the tile so you don't have to trim tiles against curved metal corners.

Counter Edging. There are several ways to trim the counter edge with tile. The most common is to install V-cap matched to the field tiles. It creates a neat border with no grout joint at the outer edge, and it covers the backer board and plywood. You also can use bullnose tiles along the edge or even a strip of wood.

Backsplashes. Most counter layouts include a backsplash. Take its thickness into account when planning the countertop field: the tiles themselves on drywall, or tiles plus a backer board (and plywood, too, in some cases) in wet areas. You also can use tiles with a cove base to make an easy-cleaning seam.

Ceramic and stone tile complement other building materials. Here, stone tiles form a backsplash behind a dark granite countertop.

COUNTERTOP CONSTRUCTION

FRONT EDGE OPTIONS

Wood Trim

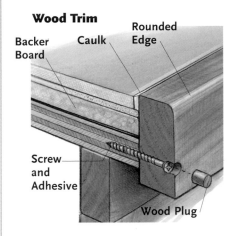

Backer Board
Caulk
Rounded Edge
Screw and Adhesive
Wood Plug

Bullnose Tile

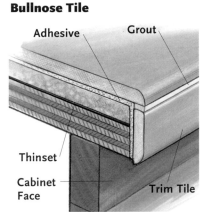

Adhesive
Grout
Thinset
Cabinet Face
Trim Tile

V-Cap Tile

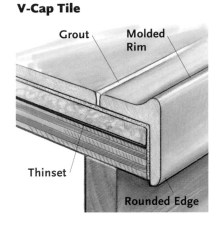

Grout
Molded Rim
Thinset
Rounded Edge

COUNTERTOP OPTIONS

Dry-Area Thinset

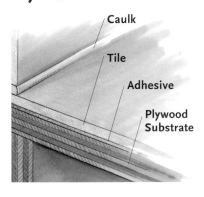

Caulk
Tile
Adhesive
Plywood Substrate

Wet-Area Thickset

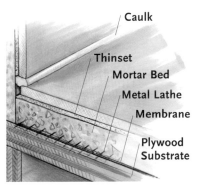

Caulk
Thinset
Mortar Bed
Metal Lathe
Membrane
Plywood Substrate

Wet-Area Thinset

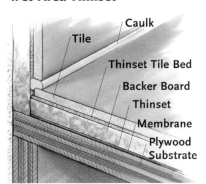

Caulk
Tile
Thinset Tile Bed
Backer Board
Thinset
Membrane
Plywood Substrate

BACKSPLASH OPTIONS

Capped Top

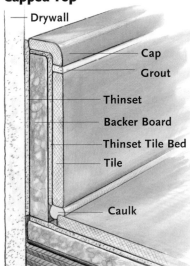

Drywall
Cap
Grout
Thinset
Backer Board
Thinset Tile Bed
Tile
Caulk

Coved Base

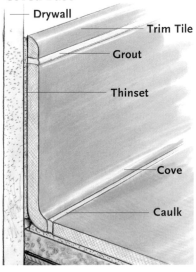

Drywall
Trim Tile
Grout
Thinset
Cove
Caulk

Bullnose Return

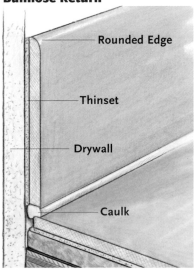

Rounded Edge
Thinset
Drywall
Caulk

Tiling Countertops

project

You can apply tile over an existing countertop as long as the surface is smooth and sound, but in most cases you will need to add a layer of plywood or backer board. For a new countertop, start by applying a layer of ¾-inch plywood reinforced with support strips of wood followed by a layer of backer board. The backer board provides a smooth, flat surface for the tile. While it is not waterproof, it will not be damaged should it get wet.

TOOLS & MATERIALS

- Table or circular saw ▍Plywood ▍Drill and screws ▍Glue and construction adhesive
- Staple gun and staples ▍Utility knife
- 4-mil. polyethylene moisture barrier ▍Backer board ▍Fiberglass mesh tape ▍Thinset

1 Cut ¾-in.-thick plywood to size for the countertop using a circular saw or a table saw. Then cut 3-in.-wide support strips from the scrap plywood. These should be installed on the underside of the counter around the perimeter and at every seam. Also, add a support strip where the base cabinets meet.

4 Make final adjustments; then attach the counter by driving screws up through the cabinet corner braces and into the bottom of the counter. Use screws that are long enough to firmly attach the top but won't go through the surface. Have a helper hold down the counter while you are driving the screws.

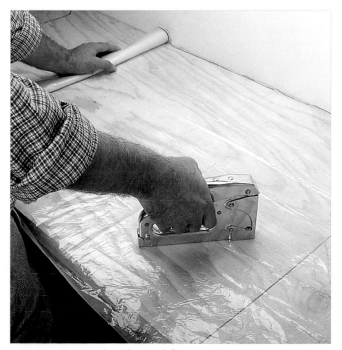

5 To protect the plywood from moisture, install a barrier between the plywood and the backer board. Cut 4-mil.-thick polyethylene to size, and staple it to the plywood. You can also use 15-lb. roofing felt as a moisture-resistant membrane.

2 The best way to attach the support strips is with yellow carpenter's glue and drywall screws. First, cut and lay out all the strips on the bottom of the counter to make sure they fit. Then spread glue on the bottom of the strips, and lower them in place. Drive drywall screws every 4 to 6 inches.

3 Once the countertop is finished, test-fit it to check for problems. Make the necessary adjustments; remove it; and then apply construction adhesive to the top of the cabinets. Apply a bead that's at least ¼ in. in diameter, and spread it slightly to make sure all areas are covered. Then lift the counter into place.

6 After you have installed the membrane, cut pieces of backer board to size; then spread thinset mortar using a notched trowel. Carefully lower each backer board panel into the thinset, leaving a ⅛-in. gap between panels. Don't spread more thinset adhesive than you can easily cover before it starts to set.

7 Use fiberglass mesh tape to help bind the edges of the backer board and plywood. Also use this tape to finish the gaps between the backer-board panels. To do this, spread thinset in the gaps; cut the tape pieces to size; and embed them in the thinset. Use a putty knife to do this as you would finish a drywall joint.

PREPPING FOR A SINK INSTALLATION

Be sure that the cutout location leaves enough room to run supply pipes between the sink and the back of the cabinet.

TOOLS & MATERIALS

▌ Measuring tape and framing square ▌ Marker or pencil ▌ Drill and ¾-in. bit ▌ Saber saw ▌ 4-mil polyethylene ▌ Staple gun ▌ Notched trowel ▌ Thinset and backer board ▌ Fiberglass mesh tape

1 Measure carefully to center the cutout. Remember to figure only interior, front-to-back cabinet space where the sink will be housed.

4 Follow the cut line, working slowly at corners where you rotate the saw. Support the cutout below or install a top cleat as you finish the cut.

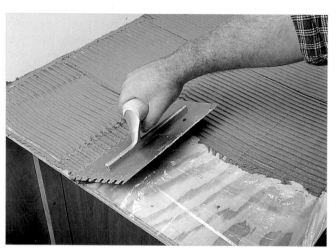

5 Lay a moisture membrane such as 4-mil. polyethylene over the plywood. Then trowel on a bed of thinset adhesive using a notched trowel.

Thorough prep work leads to a professional-quality installation. Notice the tile detail around the rim of the sink.

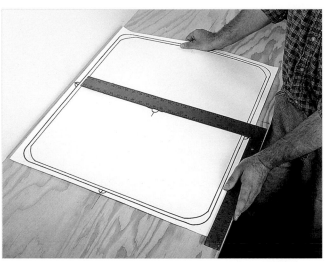

2 Use a template with a framing square to position the cutout. If you trace the sink outline, measure in from the lip overhang to mark the actual cut line.

3 Although some saber saws are capable of a plunge cut, it's best to drill a starter hole. Make sure the hole is just inside your cut line.

6 Install sheets of cement backer board up to the edges of the cutout using corrosion-resistant screws. Add narrow strips front and back.

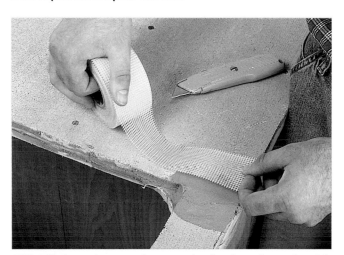

7 Fill the ⅛-in. gaps between backer board panels with thinset, and embed a layer of fiberglass mesh tape over all the panel seams.

SUPPORTING THE CUTOUT

WHEN YOU CUT A SINK OPENING in ¾-inch-thick plywood, the surrounding wood will support the cut for most of the job. But as your saw heads back to the starting point, the cutout section will start to sag. The blade may bind, and the cut piece may tear.

Solve these problems with a temporary cleat. It should be long enough to cover the cut section plus an inch or so on each side. Two screws will hold the cut section to the cleat, and the ends of the cleat will hold the cutout flush with the counter.

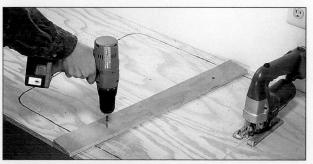

A temporary cleat keeps the sink cutout from falling and causing a ragged break.

Tiling Countertops

INSTALLING FIELD TILES

project

To lay out a new countertop, snap guide lines to indicate the placement of your edging tiles. If the counter will include a row of partial tiles, make a dry run with the tiles and spacers to determine the best layout. As always, try to minimize the number of cuts. If you choose a wood (rather then tile) edging, plan for the field tiles along the front of the counter to be flush with the edge of the counter. No matter what the situation, always use full tiles along the front and place partial tiles along the back.

TOOLS & MATERIALS

▌ Edge tiles ▌ Chalk-line box with red chalk
▌ Field tiles ▌ Adhesive ▌ Notched trowel
▌ Tile spacers ▌ Framing square

1 To locate the front line of the countertop field tiles, hold a trim tile against the counter edge and mark its edge in several spots. This will take into account any slight irregularities in the edge of the counter.

SCRIBING TO AN UNEVEN WALL

FEW WALLS in old (and new) houses are perfectly straight and square to other walls. In most cases, these problems aren't visible because most of them show up where the wall meets the floor or the ceiling, where few of us look. But sometimes the problems are so bad that they are noticeable and must be accommodated. If you are doing an entire remodel, remove the wallboard; diagnose the problem; and fix it. But if you can't do this, another option is to scribe the materials to fit the wall.

There are a couple of ways to do this. But the easiest and most accurate way is to use a small, inexpensive compass like the one that every geometry student has used. This V-shaped tool consists of two legs, one has a metal point on the end, the other holds a pencil. To use this tool, just slide the point leg along the wall and hold the pencil leg against the workpiece. It will trace the shape of the wall exactly, as long as you hold the tool in the same position as you move along the wall. When the scribe is complete, cut the workpiece.

Keep the compass points aligned as you mark the contour of the wall onto the plywood.

2 Snap a chalk line to establish the location of the trim tiles and the first row of field tiles. Remember to include the grout joint in your calculations. Because the tile adhesive will cover part of the lines, use red chalk because it reads better than blue chalk and is worth using on this job.

3 Once the layout is worked out and the chalk lines are snapped, start spreading the adhesive. Use a notched trowel sized to the instructions on the adhesive package. Work in small areas to avoid having the adhesive set before the tiles are installed. If you have an L-shaped counter, start where the two legs meet.

4 Start at the front of the counter with full-size field tiles. Carefully lower each tile into the adhesive. Then twist it slightly from side to side before pressing it down firmly. Use tile spacers to keep the grout joints uniform. If adhesive gets on the face of any tile, remove it before installing more tiles.

5 Continue installing the rest of the full-size tiles and their spacers. Be sure to check for alignment in both directions. Use a framing square to check for square with the front edge of the counter and a long straightedge to make sure the tiles lie flat.

Tiling Countertops

INSTALLING PARTIAL TILES AND EDGING

If your installation is square, you can make all the partial tiles along your backsplash the same size. But on some jobs, especially when you are tiling over an existing counter, the top will not be square. In other words, it will be wider at one end than the other. Because of this, it's wise to check the counter depth at several points along the top to see whether any adjustments are required. If you find a problem, cut the tiles one by one to match the space they'll occupy.

TOOLS & MATERIALS

▮ Full tiles and edging tiles ▮ Pencil ▮ Tile spacers ▮ Snap tile cutter ▮ Notched trowel and putty knife ▮ Adhesive ▮ Fiberglass mesh tape ▮ Putty knives ▮ Wet saw

1 To mark the cut line for a partial tile, place a full tile over the last full field tile; butt it against the backsplash; and mark where the two tiles meet. Then, measure the width of a grout joint, and deduct this from the scribed line on your partial tile. Make a new cut line mark.

4 Install tile spacers on the full tiles that are already in place. Then press a partial tile into the adhesive, and twist it slightly to make sure it seats thoroughly. Check for proper joint alignment, and continue on to the other tiles. Work carefully but quickly to reduce the chance of the adhesive drying before the tiles are installed.

5 Place fiberglass mesh tape on the edge of the counter, and spread adhesive over it using a notched trowel. Then cover the back of an edge tile with adhesive using a putty knife. Apply it so that it's about ⅛ in. thick. Press the edge tile against the counter (inset), and slide it slightly from side to side to seat it completely.

2 Slide the marked tile into a snap cutter, and push it against the fence. Score the glaze on the tile. Then push the handle back to the fence (without moving the tile), and press the handle down. The tile will break into two pieces.

3 Remove any dust, debris, and old adhesive from the surface of the counter; then spread new adhesive on the counter using a notched putty knife. Make sure to apply enough adhesive so the partial tiles will bond properly. Avoid smearing excess adhesive on the surface of the installed tiles.

6 The edge tiles that form an inside corner on the counter must be mitered to fit properly and look attractive. Unfortunately, not every L-shaped counter has perfect 90-deg. corners. If it is square, then cut the tile at a 45-deg. angle. If it's not square, bisect the angle, and cut the corner tiles to this angle.

7 Place one of the mitered corner tiles on the counter. Make sure it fits properly, then push it into the adhesive. Cut the second tile; check it for fit; and install it. Use tile spacers to maintain even grout joints with the field tile. The grout joint between the mitered tiles should also match the width of a standard grout joint.

Tiling Countertops

MAKING A COUNTERTOP BACKSPLASH

There are several ways to build a counter-top backsplash. One is to install the counter and its tile first. Then build the backsplash in place by screwing backer board to the wall and mounting the tile directly to this substrate. Or construct the backsplash as part of the countertop, and install the tile as part of the countertop project. To simplify the job, make sure that the backsplash is the same size as a whole tile, or two whole tiles.

TOOLS & MATERIALS

▌ ¾-in.-thick exterior-grade plywood
▌ Circular saw or table saw ▌ Wood glue and screws ▌ Caulk and caulking gun
▌ Drill with countersink and screwdriver bits ▌ Clamps ▌ Utility knife

1 Using a table saw or a circular with a rip fence, cut 3-in.-wide strips of ¾-in.-thick plywood to reinforce the back edge of the countertop.

4 Carefully press the backsplash to the counter, and support it in place as you install clamps to hold it. Make sure that the bottom edge of the splash is flush with the bottom surface of the counter. Once the clamps are tight, a bead of silicone caulk should squeeze out of the entire length of the joint.

5 Use a countersink bit to bore pilot holes for the screws that attach the splash to the counter. These bits are a combination of a drill bit that bores a hole for the screw and a countersink bit for cutting a recessed hole for the screwhead. This ensures that the screwheads will be recessed below the surface of the panel.

2 Attach the support strips to the underside of the counter using carpenter's glue and screws. Make sure the screws are shorter than the thickness of the two layers of plywood. Also, make sure that the outside edge of the counter and the support strip are smooth and flush to each other.

3 Cut the backsplash panel to size; then draw a line that shows where the back of the counter falls. Apply a thick bead of silicone caulk to the area between the bottom of the backsplash and the line. Then spread it with a putty knife so that the area is filled to a uniform thickness. Silicone protects the joint from exposure to moisture.

6 Using a drill, drive the screws into the holes. Install one every 5 to 6 in., and make sure that the caulk squeezes out along the joint. If it doesn't in some areas, add an extra screw or two to tighten the joint. If you don't get the caulk to squeeze out for the entire length of the joint, apply a bead from above.

7 Once the caulk has cured, cut through it from the top and the bottom with a sharp utility knife. Then peel the caulk away from the joint, and slide the assembled counter onto the base cabinets. Attach it with screws driven up through the cabinet corner blocks into the bottom of the counter.

Tiling Countertops

ONE TILE & CAP

The easiest and quickest installation uses the same basic grid as the countertop tiles, and simply extends the grid one course onto the wall. Remember to leave a standard-width seam between the backsplash and the counter. Where you may get some movement between the two components, use caulk in this joint instead of grout.

Dry-Area Prep Work. In dry areas you can apply tile adhesive directly to the drywall and set the tile in place.

Wet-Area Prep Work. In wet areas, cut backer board to fit the tile and cap; comb the back of the panel with thin-set; and screw with corrosion-resistant fasteners to the wall studs.

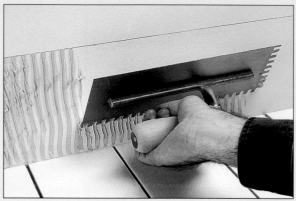

1 Use a notched trowel to spread adhesive from the counter to a top guideline on the wall. You can add tape to keep a clean line.

MULTIPLE ROWS & CAP

Use multiple rows of tile or combinations of sizes and shapes that create a decorative accent for the countertop. Some tiles are sold in decorative sets, such as a group of four pretrimmed tiles designed to fit around a center medallion. Square-edged tiles in sets need a cap tile on the top row.

Color Contrast. If you change color between the countertop and the backsplash, maintain the same grout spacing to tie the areas together. Create a more decorative look by using contrasting colors within the backsplash grid—for example, by matching the counter color with the medallion tile.

Spacing. If tiles tend to sag on the adhesive, use temporary spacers to maintain spacing.

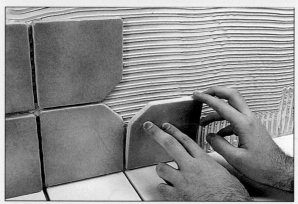

1 Install pattern sets, pretrimmed for insert tiles, to create a more decorative backsplash. Inserts have to be centered to maintain grout spacing.

MULTIPLE TRIM STRIPS

When you begin to combine basic elements, such as single rows and tile sets with accents, you can create many variations. You can add contrasting colors to the mix and decorative tiles with an embossed pattern or picture. More complex layouts call for careful planning. Larger backsplash installations can also support intermediate trim strips.

Dry Layout. Test your design with a dry layout. You can temporarily tape sample pieces to a board so that you can see how the design looks on the wall.

Staggering Joints. Lining up vertical grout seams on a large backsplash emphasizes height. Offsetting intermediate trim strips so that they bridge the seams between full tiles emphasizes width.

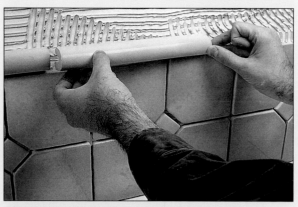

1 Intermediate trim strips separate different design elements on a backsplash wall. They also tie together different colors and shapes.

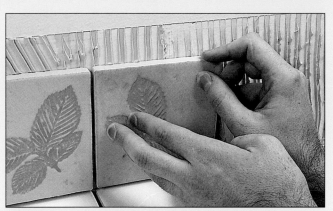

2 Set the row of backsplash tiles into the adhesive, but leave a standard seam along the bottom. You may need spacers to keep the tiles from sagging.

3 Cover the top edges of full backsplash tiles with a cap tile. Another option is to use tile with a finished, bullnose edge on top.

2 Press pattern inserts into place by hand. You may want to use a straightedge to make sure they are flush with the surrounding tiles.

3 A larger backsplash with a more complex pattern can support a larger, S-shaped cap. You also can make caps from cut sections of bullnose tiles.

2 Horizontal trim strips provide a secondary baseline to support a row of decorative tiles with different colors and patterns.

3 When you combine different design elements, it generally looks best to use narrow trim strips in the pattern and wide trim on the cap.

FINISHING A BACKSPLASH

project

Some backsplashes are relatively short, while others fill the entire wall from the top of the counter to the bottom of the wall cabinets. Regardless of the size, the finishing approach remains the same. The tile joints need to be filled with grout; the excess grout has to be cleaned away; and the finished surface of the grout should be sealed to protect it from stains and water damage. Use the grout that is recommended by the tile manufacturer.

TOOLS & MATERIALS

▌Narrow screwdriver or chisel ▌Rubber-faced grout float and squeegee ▌Drywall taping knife ▌Grout striking tool ▌Sponge, rags, and bucket ▌Silicone sealer

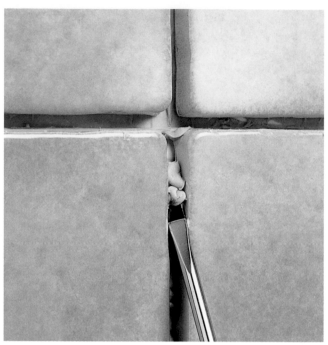

1 Check all the grout joints for tile adhesive that squeezed out doing the installation process. Use a narrow, flat-blade screwdriver to remove this adhesive, or you can use a narrow-blade chisel as long as you approach the job carefully. Use a shop vac or a paint-brush to remove the fine dust.

4 Once all the joints are full, remove excess grout from the surface before it dries using a damp rag or a window washer's squeegee. Wipe this tool clean after each stroke, and take care to remove the grout just from the surface of the tiles. Don't force it out of the joints.

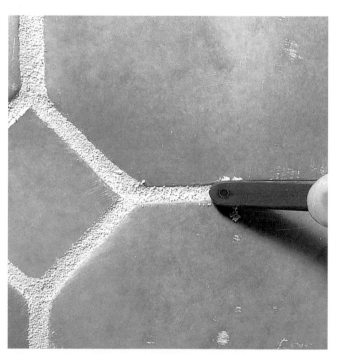

5 To achieve the most uniform grout joints, it's a good idea to strike the joints using a narrow rounded object like the end of a toothbrush, as shown here, or a wood dowel. The goal is to trim the grout until it just reaches the bottom edge of the glaze that's baked on the surface.

2 Mix the dry grout with water to the consistency recommended on the product container. Then use a drywall knife to load the grout onto a rubber-faced grout float. Cover about half of the float with grout. If you spread more onto this tool, it usually will fall off the float when you try to spread it on the wall.

3 Apply the grout using diagonal strokes beginning at the bottom of the splash and moving toward the top. This direction means that most of the grout that falls will drop back on the float, not onto the counter. As you apply the grout, press the float firmly against the tiles to force the grout deep into the joints.

6 After all the grout joints are struck and you're satisfied with the way they look, wipe the surface of the backsplash to remove any grout fragments and to clean away the haze that the grout leaves behind. Use a damp sponge, not a dripping wet one, and rinse it in clean water after each pass.

7 Once the grout is set, which usually takes at least 24 hours, buff the surface with a clean cloth to remove the faint haze that is almost always left behind. Then protect the grout with a liquid silicone sealer that comes in an easy-to-use applicator bottle. Just press the tip against the joint to apply the sealer.

INSTALLING A GLASS-TILE BACKSPLASH

Using glass tile on a countertop backsplash is a great way to add some life to your kitchen without spending a great deal of money. True, the glass tiles themselves are comparatively expensive, usually three to four times the price of common ceramic tiles. But when glass tiles are used as accents, as they are here, or as trim pieces, the cost is much more reasonable.

These tiles are interesting because they absorb and reflect light differently than standard glazed tiles. As a result they can appear to shimmer or vibrate slightly when you look at them from different angles.

Glass tiles are commonly available in 2x2 and 4x4 sizes and in a wide variety of mosaic sheets that range from subtle to overwhelming with many stops in between. A local tile store or home center will have a good selection from which to choose. But keep in mind that these stores sell a lot more ceramic tile than they do glass tile, so it is not unusual for the retailer to special order what you want.

Glass tiles not only look different, but they're also made differently, out of glass instead of clay. Because of this, they have a few special installation requirements. The first is that the mastic must be a white, latex reinforced mortar, not the standard thinset mortar used for ceramic tile. The reason for this is two-fold. First, the glass surface doesn't bond well to the standard mortar. Second, the mastic can be seen through the tile when the job is done. Using gray-colored thinset dulls the color of the tile. The hue of the mastic is not the only thing that is visible through the tile. The trowel marks can also be seen. That's why the standard installation approach is to back-butter (coat the back of) each glass tile before it is installed so that no air bubbles or notched trowel grooves appear.

Some glass-tile manufacturers have eliminated the need for back buttering by applying a white coating to the tile so that neither the color nor the grooves of the mastic can show through. The photo below shows just how effective this can be.

Wall Preparation

The best approach on any tile job is to minimize the cutting required. In this case, because the backsplash was located behind a freestanding range, it was easy to use mostly standard-sized tiles. We worked out a design then laid the tiles on a workbench with the spacers in place and measured the overall size.

Renting a tile saw is required. Or you can buy an inexpensive model, especially if you plan to do more tile work in the future.

If you are installing tiles on part of the wall, as in the project shown opposite, install a guide board to support the first row of tiles.

INSTALLING GLASS TILES IN A BACKSPLASH

project

Check with the tile manufacturer to determine which type mastic to use. Most require a white mastic because the tiles are transparent and will show whatever is beneath them, including the gray color of most thinset and the grooves created by the trowel. Some tiles come with a white backing. Freshly cut glass tiles can have extremely sharp edges. Be sure to wear leather gloves when handling these cut tiles.

TOOLS & MATERIALS

▮ Ceramic and glass tiles ▮ Tile spacers
▮ Measuring tape ▮ Level ▮ 1-by support board ▮ Electric drill ▮ Work gloves ▮ Electric wet saw ▮ Smoothing stone ▮ White latex-reinforced thinset mortar ▮ Notched trowel ▮ Putty knife ▮ Grout float ▮ Sponge

1 Pre-assemble the backsplash tiles on a flat surface to check for proper spacing and to measure the size on any tiles that need to be cut. By completing this layout before the mortar is on the wall, you won't feel rushed to install the tiles before the mortar sets. Once everything fits, measure the height and width of the assembly.

2 Make any necessary cuts with an electric wet tile saw. This tool is essential for cutting glass tiles and makes cutting ceramic tiles much faster and cleaner. It's a common rental item that usually costs about $40–$50 per day. You can also buy an inexpensive model for less than $100.

3 Once a tile is cut, smooth the edge using a smoothing stone that's available at tile stores and home centers. One side has a coarse grit while the other side has a fine grit. Smoothing the cut edges of glass tiles is absolutely necessary. If left unsmoothed, the cut glass edge can be sharper than a knife's blade.

Continued on next page. **129**

Tiling Countertops

Continued from previous page.

4 Use a level to lay out the position of the backsplash on the wall. Here, two base lines were required: one for the bottom edge of the first row of tiles and another for the bottom edge of the backer board. This was necessary because the trim tiles that surround the glass tiles cover the edge of the backer board on all four sides.

5 Screw a guide board for the bottom row of tiles to the wall. Make sure the top edge of the board aligns precisely with the layout line. Using screws makes removing the board later easier. Drill pilot holes for these screws to make driving the screws and maintaining proper alignment much easier.

8 Begin installing the tile by resting the bottom trim tiles on the guide board and pressing each into the mastic. Move the tile slightly from side to side to make sure the back is completely embedded in the mastic. Use small tile spacers to maintain proper alignment. Once a tile is installed, avoid disturbing it until the mastic cures.

9 These 4x4 glass tiles are installed just like standard ceramic tiles. Place each on top of the course below, and press carefully but firmly into the mastic. Use tile spacers to maintain alignment, and wipe away any mastic from the surface of the tiles before it starts to cure. If it dries on the surface, it's much harder to remove.

6 Install the cement backer board that creates a stable base for the tiles. This material is easy to cut. Just score it with a utility knife, and snap it like you would a piece of drywall. Use corrosion-resistant screws that are designed for this job. Attach the board to all studs using 4- to 5-in. spacing.

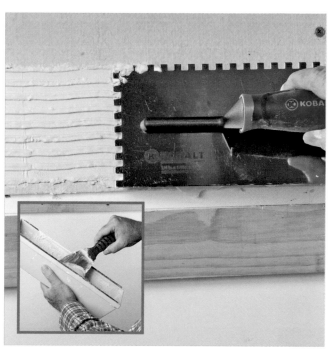

7 Apply mastic to the wall using a notched trowel. Strive for uniform coverage, and work in small areas so you'll have time to install the tiles before the mastic starts to set. Because this job required only small batches of mastic, a drywall joint compound pan was used to make the mix (inset).

10 Press each ceramic tile with an insert opening into the mastic. Then carefully install the matching accent glass tile. Maintain proper spacing around the accent tile using wood toothpicks, making sure to remove them before the mastic cures. Work carefully because errors will be visible once the grout is installed.

11 Once all the tiles are installed and the mastic properly cured, fill the tile joints with grout. Spread it across the surface using a rubber-faced grout trowel. Firmly force the grout into each joint until it's full. Finish up by wiping away excess grout with a damp but not soaking wet sponge (inset).

INSTALLING A MOSAIC TILE VANITY TOP

Most common mosaic tiles come in sheets, often 12 inches square, with the individual tiles glued to a mesh backer. This makes installing these small tiles much easier. The job goes quicker because of the size of the sheets, and it looks better because the grout joints are so consistent. Except for this mesh backer, mosaics are generally installed the same way as other ceramic tiles. You begin with a cement-backer-board base, followed by a coat of thinset mortar. You then lay the tiles in the mortar; when the mortar is dry, you fill the gaps between the tiles with grout.

MOSAIC TILE VANITY TOP

Tile vanity tops sometimes omit a tiled back-splash. A good replacement is a straight piece of knot-free pine.

TOOLS & MATERIALS

▌Backer board ▌Saber saw ▌Power drill, screws ▌Edge trim tiles ▌Tape ▌Mosaic tile sheets ▌Notched trowel ▌Thinset ▌Tile nippers ▌Scrap wood block and hammer ▌Rubber-faced trowel ▌Grout

Mosaic Tile Layout

Layout is just as important for mosaics as it is for other types of tile. Because this freestanding vanity had plenty of room around it, we laid out our counter to fit the tile instead of the other way around. By just adding ½ inch to the width and depth of the top, we were able to use standard edge trim pieces and full tiles across the top. This saved a lot of cutting and made for a much better-looking job.

Once your tile installation is complete, reinstall the vanity sink. Before dropping it in place, run a thick bead of clear silicone caulk around the perimeter of the sink cut-out. Drop the sink in place. Let the caulk dry; then trim excess caulk flush to the sink using a utility knife.

1 Remove the existing sink, and cover the vanity top with a piece of cement backer board. Mark and cut out the sink opening using a saber saw.

4 Carefully install the edge tiles first, starting at the corners. The grout lines on the edge tiles should match those of the mosaic sheets.

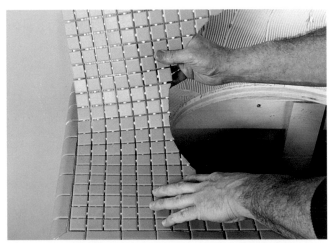

5 Start installing the mosaic sheets at the perimeter, and work toward the sink hole. Carefully lower the sheet into the mortar.

INSTALLING BROKEN MOSAIC TILES

To create your own distinctive mosaic tiles, just put a variety of different colored tile into a plastic storage bag, and break them with a hammer. Try for pieces that are about 1 in. wide.

Spread some thinset mortar on your vanity top, and push the broken tile into the mortar in a random pattern. Keep the top as flat as possible to make grouting easier later.

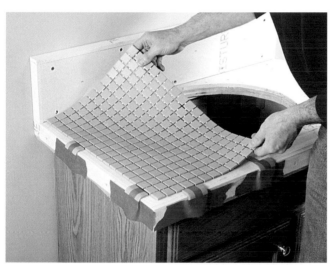

2 Temporarily tape a few trim pieces in place; then determine the most attractive layout for the mosaic tile.

3 Spread thinset mortar on the edges and top of the backer board. Apply the mortar uniformly, following the manufacturer's directions.

6 Once all the sheets are installed, carefully tap the sheets into the mortar using a scrap wood block and a rubber mallet or hammer.

7 Once the mortar has cured, mix up some tile grout according to the manufacturer's directions. Spread it over the tiles using a rubber trowel.

design ideas

Stone tiles, opposite, contain colorful mosaic-tile insets to add sparkle to this short backsplash.

Light-brown tiles, left, work well with this cream-colored vanity.

Speciality tiles, below left, allow you to decorate backsplashes with unique themes, such as this scene of man's best friend.

Glass tiles, below, complement a sophisticated design. The colors in the tiles change slightly in different light levels.

Tiling Countertops

design ideas

Tile landing spot, below, inset next to a range.

Elegant tile design, right, complements a distinctive faucet.

Distinctive trim tiles, below, enhance a vanity top.

Colorful tiles, opposite, used on a counter and backsplash.

Tiling Countertops

Mosaic tiles, below, add a rich appealing touch to a makeup vanity. Note the curved edge to the left of the photo.

Green and white tiles, right, combine to set the tone for this retro bathroom.

A distinctive vanity top, below right, helps set the mood in this powder room.

Distinctive stone tiles, opposite, are used to create an unusual vanity area.

tiling tubs and showers

6

FEW MATERIALS are as suitable for showers and tub surrounds as tile. Smooth, highly glazed tiles are easy to clean, and they can stand up to abrasive and chemical cleaners. For a long-lasting installation, both the tile and backing must be watertight. For maximum protection against seepage, use a water-resistant adhesive such as latex thinset. Where tile joins a tub, you need the stability and water resistance of cement-based backer board on the surrounding walls.

Tiling Tubs and Showers

project

REMOVING OLD TILE

When you are remodeling an existing room, the conditions can be challenging. Usually, the first step is to remove the old tile and either the thick bed of mortar, the cement backer board, or the drywall that is underneath. This is always a demanding and messy job. The shards of broken tile are sharp and fly around freely when they are chipped off the wall. Because of this, be sure to wear work gloves, a dust mask, eye goggles, a cap, long pants, work boots, and a thick long-sleeve shirt.

TOOLS & MATERIALS

▪ Power drill and masonry bit ▪ Sledge hammer or heavy framing hammer
▪ Cold chisel ▪ Pry bar ▪ Large bucket

1 Sometimes it's difficult to get a start with a cold chisel because the blade tends to skip over the surface. To create a good point of entry, drill a series of holes through the face of a single tile; then strike the tile with a hammer along this line of holes. The tile should shatter and provide an edge for the chisel to grip.

INVESTIGATING WATER DAMAGE

CRACKED GROUT, extensive mold stains, loose tiles, and a surface that flexes when you push on it are all indicators of water damage behind the tile. Sometimes you can pop off the loose tile, let the surface dry, and re-tile the area. But when damage is more than skin-deep, you need to investigate further. Often you won't see dampness on the surface. But if you remove the loose tile, and find damp or spongy drywall underneath, you'll have to keep digging until everything is dry and there is no apparent damage. If the wall framing is rotten, unfortunately, you'll have to replace the framing and install new backer board and tile.

Scrape a sharp knife across a damp and discolored stud. If the wood surface is sound underneath, let the stud dry out, and leave it in place.

Dig in the point of a knife to see whether the wood is rotten. If you can dig out crumbling wood, the best course of action is to replace the stud.

2 Once the cold chisel has a tile edge to work against, place the blade where the back of the tile meets the substrate, and strike it with a hammer or maul. Vary the angle until you find what works best. The goal is to chip off the tile and the mortar at the same time.

3 In many cases, using a flat pry bar is a better choice for removing the tile. Drive the flat end under a tile, and pull up. The tile generally comes off as a single piece, instead of in pieces, so the job isn't as messy nor as danger-ous. But whole tiles can hurt if they hit your feet. So wear heavy work boots while doing this, or any, demolition work.

4 Typically, drywall is installed with screws. So have a drill with a Phillips bit close at hand to remove any exposed screws. On older jobs, however, drywall panels were nailed to the house framing. You can pull these nails with a flat pry bar, nail puller, or the claws of a standard carpenter's hammer.

5 Once the tile and most of the mortar are removed, strip the walls of the drywall panels. Use a flat pry bar, a wrecking bar, and a heavy carpenter's hammer. Once part of each panel is loose, you can often break off the rest in large pieces. Then finish the demolition by removing the fasteners that were left behind.

ENCLOSURE CONSTRUCTION

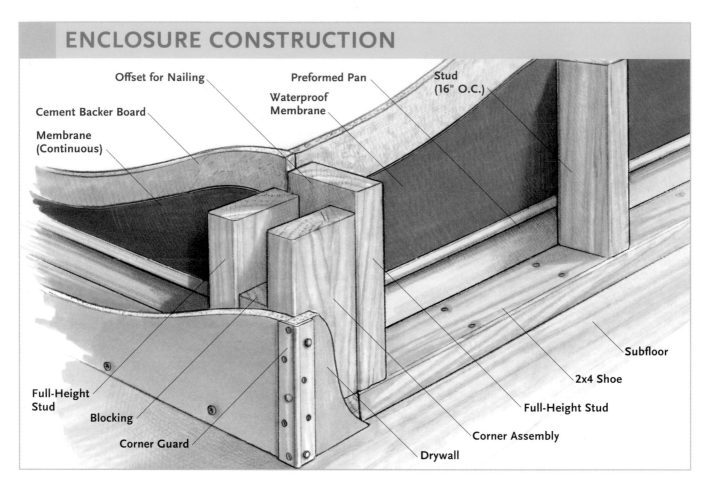

Offset for Nailing

Preformed Pan

Waterproof
Membrane

Stud
(16" O.C.)

Cement Backer Board

Membrane
(Continuous)

Subfloor

2x4 Shoe

Full-Height
Stud

Blocking

Full-Height Stud

Corner Assembly

Corner Guard

Drywall

PLANNING THE JOB

If you are building a shower stall or bathtub enclosure from scratch, the easiest approach is to install a prefabricated shower pan. With showers, you can use a pan (usually made of fiberglass) that has a hole for the drain connections and short walls with flanges. Set the pan in the enclosure, and install backer board on the walls that rest on top of the flanges. With tubs, you may need to pack a bedding material (usually a fast-setting, lightweight plaster) around the tub base to stabilize the unit and prevent flexing.

Tiling a Shower Pan

If you want to tile a shower floor as well as the walls, you can buy a pre-tiled pan or build your own base with a mortar bed that slopes to the drain. Mortar installations are troweled over a waterproof membrane. You can install a mortar bed over an exterior-grade plywood subfloor or use concrete over an existing slab. For a do-it-yourselfer with limited experience, it's wise to have an experienced contractor install the pan.

Closing Off the Shower

You can try to keep water in a shower enclosure simply by hanging a curtain across the opening. But most showers look better and leak less with a fitted glass door. This approach does make tiling more complicated.

Generally you need to build stub walls on either side of the opening and a curb along the front edge. Stub walls are framed in before the tile and backing are installed. They make a neat opening but create more tiled corners and edges than a basic tiled box closed off with a curtain.

Although some shower doors can be adjusted slightly for width, you need to plan a door opening very carefully. The framing has to leave room for a layer of backer board and tile. In the stub framing, include a curb that rises higher than the pan itself. The overall height of the opening normally isn't crucial, because you don't need to close in the top of the door. But try to plan the curb height to minimize the number of cuts and partial tiles.

If you decide not to use stub walls, the front edge of the fiberglass pan serves as a threshold to contain water. In every case, it's wise to set blocks of framing and backer board in place and try a test layout.

ENCLOSURE FLOOR MEMBRANES

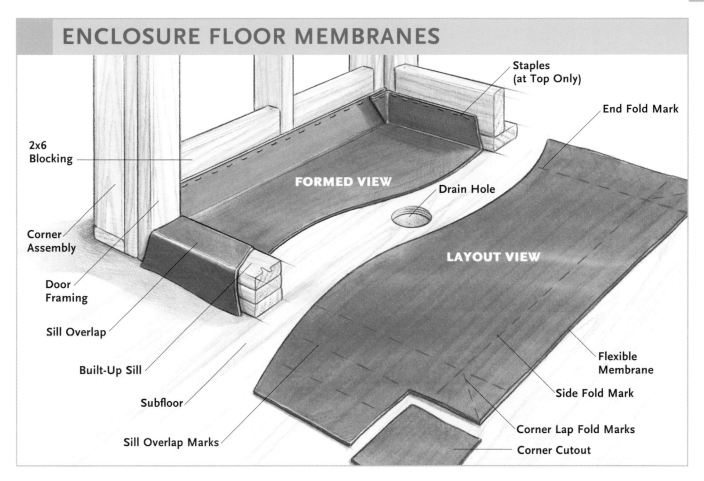

Designing the Enclosure

In conventional tub and shower surrounds, the tile usually extends from the top edges of the tub or shower pan to 6 or 8 inches above the showerhead. Of course, you can tile all the way to the ceiling, too. Around tubs without showerheads, you can install a tiled backsplash extending a foot or two above the tub.

In situations where the walls extend beyond the sides of the tub and you do not want to tile the entire wall, you'll need to edge the installation with bullnose tile. This is a good spot to add an extra strip of trim tiles. For example, you might add several rows of full tiles extending up from the edge of the tub, and top them with narrow trim strips in a contrasting color before adding another row of full tiles and bullnose trim.

Instead of aligning the outermost row with the edge of the tub, it often looks neater to extend the backsplash along the wall by a tile or two, and run those columns of tiles down to floor level.

Tiling the ceiling is best left to a professional who will use fast-setting adhesives and plywood forms supported by long props to hold the tiles until the adhesive cures.

Stub walls and a raised threshold provide support for shower doors.

Tiling Tubs and Showers

INSTALLING A PREFAB SHOWER PAN

project

To create a custom-size shower stall, you'll have to build your own shower pan as shown on pages 148 and 149. But if a standard-size stall works for your plan, you should use a prefab shower pan. These one-piece units are much easier to install, and they are virtually leak-proof—as long as you install the drain plumbing correctly, the walls are square and plumb, and the floor is level.

TOOLS & MATERIALS

▮ Framing square ▮ Prefab shower pan and drain ▮ Pencil ▮ Saber saw ▮ Measuring tape and level ▮ Drill, screwdriver bit, and screws ▮ 2x6s for blocking ▮ Rubber mallet ▮ Backer board, thinset mortar, and fiberglass tape

1 Inspect the wall studs with a framing square to check for square construction. If the enclosure area is square and the studs are plumb, you can begin installing the pan. But if there are problems, adjust the framing for the shower so that it is square and plumb.

4 Place the shower pan over the floor hole, and check for alignment. Also check that the rim of the pan is level. But if there are problems, you can level the pan using cedar shimming shingles. Just place the shingles where necessary; staple them to the floor; and cut away any excess parts that aren't needed for the leveling.

5 Prefab shower pans are constructed with a lip that does two things. First, it provides a means for attaching the pan to the studs. Second, the lip is designed to fit behind the wall covering and acts as flashing to prevent water leaks. For extra support, install 2x6 blocks between the studs, and screw the lip into these blocks.

2 Once the enclosure framing is acceptable, place the shower pan on the floor; position it according to the directions that come with the unit; and trace the circumference of the drain hole onto to the floor. If you are installing the pan over an existing drain opening, center the drain hole over the opening, and make sure it fits properly.

3 Remove the shower pan, and drill a blade-access hole in the plywood flooring. Then use a saber saw, or a reciprocating saw, to cut the opening just on the waste side of the line. Use a fine-tooth blade to get a smooth cut, and sand away any rough spots using coarse sandpaper.

6 The watertight transition from the shower pan to the plumbing drain piping is accomplished with a rubber drain gasket. The directions that come with your pan will explain how to install your specific gasket. But generally, all that's required is to drive the unit into the drain hole using a soft face hammer or mallet. Then install the drain plate.

7 Once you have installed the pan, cover the walls with cement-based backer board. Be sure to use corrosion-resistant screws or nails made for this job. After all the panels are attached, cover the joints with self-sticking fiberglass tape; then start installing the tile. Generally, tiles are installed with thinset mortar applied with a notched trowel.

INSTALLING A MORTAR-BED SHOWER FLOOR

project

For support, install blocking between the surrounding wall studs. Build a wood curb made of three 2x4s to form the front of the shower base. And finally, add blocking between all the joists that run under the shower or double up the joists. Install the drain and all below-floor plumbing lines as necessary.

TOOLS & MATERIALS

▮ Hammer, nails, and saw ▮ Measuring tape, level, and marker ▮ Exterior-grade plywood ▮ 2x4s and 2x6s ▮ Shower-pan liner ▮ Staple gun ▮ Shower-drain assembly ▮ Utility knife ▮ Combination wrench ▮ Trowel and float ▮ Thickset and thinset mortar ▮ Reinforcing mesh ▮ Silicone sealant

1 Start by adding another layer of underlayment to the floor. Install the screws in a 4-in.-square pattern. Then build a curb across the front using 2x4s. Make sure it's square and level. Install 2x6 blocking between all the wall studs. The inside surface of these blocks must be nailed flush to the inside edge of the wall studs.

4 Use a level and a marker to establish the finished height of the mortar bed. The mortar has to be sloped from this perimeter line to the drain opening. Mix up the first layer of thickset mortar, and spread it over the membrane with a trowel. It should fill about half the height between the top of the floor and this layout line.

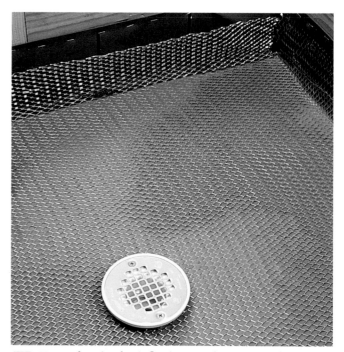

5 Use galvanized reinforcing mesh to strengthen the mortar bed. Plan for it to extend an inch or two up the side walls, and cut it to size using tin snips. Embed this mesh in the mortar before it dries. The mesh should be fitted around the drain assembly. Remove any waste at the corners so that the mesh lies flat.

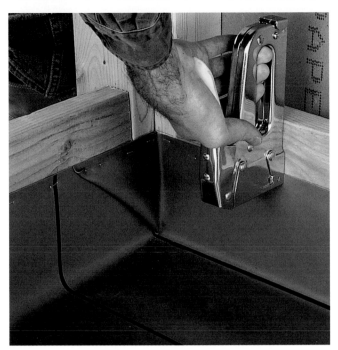

2 Once the blocking is installed, carefully cut the shower-pan liner to size, and push it against the floor. Make sure the liner is centered in the enclosure. Then start stapling along its top edge. Keep it smooth against the blocking. At corners, fold the material neatly; push it into the corner; and staple the top edge.

3 Use a utility knife to cut out the membrane over the drain opening (inset). Then attach the upper drain assembly to the lower assembly already installed in the floor. Join the two with the screws provided. Tighten the screws progressively so that the membrane is squeezed tightly and uniformly between the parts.

6 Once the mesh is in place, add the rest of the thick-set mortar to the bed. Mix this second batch to the consistency of wet sand, and spread it using a standard straightedge trowel. Then finish the surface with a large float. It will take some effort to obtain a uniform slope from the sides to the drain.

7 Allow the mortar to cure completely before moving on to the thinset mortar. Mix and spread this according to the package instructions. Use a notched trowel, and try to maintain a uniform thickness across the floor. Begin installing the tile along the walls, and move toward the drain hole.

INSTALLING TUB AND SHOWER TILE

project

Careful tile layout is always important. It improves the appearance of the job by balancing the tile spacing and can often make the job easier by reducing the number of cuts that are needed. Planning the job on paper is one thing, but making this plan work requires layout lines drawn on the walls. Begin by establishing the vertical and horizontal lines on the back wall because it is the most visible. Then extend the horizontal line to the adjacent walls.

TOOLS & MATERIALS

▌ Measuring tape and chalk-line box
▌ Level ▌ Battens and screws ▌ Power drill and screwdriver bit ▌ Thinset mortar and notched trowel ▌ Rubber grout float, spacers, and masking tape

1 Start by measuring the width of the back wall and planning a balanced layout that features end tiles that are at least half the width of a full tile. Using smaller tiles at the corners is usually considered less attractive. Once the layout is determined, locate and mark a vertical mid-line on the wall.

GREENBOARD AND BACKER BOARD

ON WALLS IN DRY LOCATIONS, like a home office or a bedroom, ceramic tile can be applied directly over standard drywall. But in damp or wet areas, like bathrooms and kitchens, a better substrate is required. In the past, green-colored water-resistant drywall (commonly called greenboard) was the product of choice. But in the last 15 or 20 years, greenboard has been fading from view and cement-based backer board has become the choice for more and more jobs. It's much heavier and harder than greenboard, and it's much more moisture resistant. These days, local building departments may prefer one over the other, so check with them before you start the job. They may also require a waterproof membrane between the wall studs and the substrate no matter which type you use. Of course, greenboard (like standard drywall) is very

In the past, water-resistant drywall was the accepted tile substrate for wet areas, but today, cement-based backer board is more commonly used.

easy to install. But backer board isn't much more difficult. You just score the cut line with a sharp utility knife, and snap the board over the edge of a worktable or against your knee. Cutting around wall obstacles such as electrical outlets is more difficult, but it's not substantially more time-consuming.

2 Mark the vertical line at the top and bottom of the wall. Then connect these marks by snapping a chalk line. Check this line for plumb with a level. If you built the enclosure carefully, this line will be level. If it's not, snap a new line that is level, and plan on installing partial tiles on the ends that are slightly tapered.

3 Use a level to find the high point of the floor. Then measure up from that point a distance that equals the height of a single tile, the grout space between tiles, and a silicone caulk joint under the bottom tile. This caulk seals the joint, making it watertight, and cushions the tile from any slight movement of the floor.

4 Extend the horizontal layout line using a level. Then draw a line along the top edge of the tool. Then move the level to the adjacent wall; line up one end with the mark on the first wall; hold the tool level; and make another mark. Do the same for the third shower wall.

5 Installing temporary battens is a good way to support the tiles while they're being installed. Screw these to the enclosure studs, and make sure that the tops of the battens are aligned precisely with the layout lines. These boards will support the tiles during installation and keep them from sagging while the mortar cures.

Continued on next page.

Tiling Tubs and Showers

Continued from previous page.

6 Begin applying the thinset mortar to the bottom of the wall. Work in small areas that you can easily cover with tiles before the adhesive dries. Use the flat edge of the trowel to apply the mortar. The goal is to get a fairly uniform layer on the entire wall.

7 Once the thinset is applied, use the notched edges of the trowel to spread it so that the wall is covered uniformly. Hold the trowel at an angle between 30 and 45 deg. to the surface. Work up to the guidelines, but not past them. If extra mortar is spread, remove it now while it's still wet. Once it's dry, it will be much harder to remove.

Careful planning allows you to create distinctive designs by combining tiles of different sizes and shapes.

8 Start installing the tile by placing the first row on the support batten. Maintain even grout lines between tiles by using small plastic tile spacers. It's easy to install the tile, but take care to maintain spacing. Little irregularities can be compounded as you move up the wall and end up noticeably distorting the grout joints.

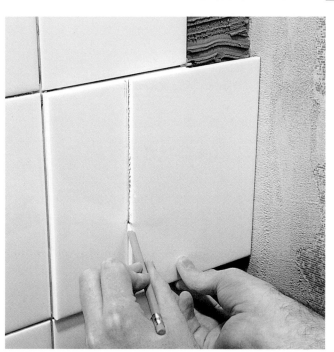

9 You can mark the cut lines on partial tiles by simply measuring the gap with a measuring tape and deducting the width of a grout joint. But it's usually faster to hold a full tile up against the last field tile to mark the cut for the corner tile. Make sure to deduct the grout joint; then make the cut with a wet saw or snap cutter.

10 When the wall tiles are installed and the mortar has cured, remove the support battens, and spread thinset on the space at the bottom of each wall. Press the tiles into place, and support each with a small piece of duct tape. Make sure to maintain uniform grout joints by using plastic spacers.

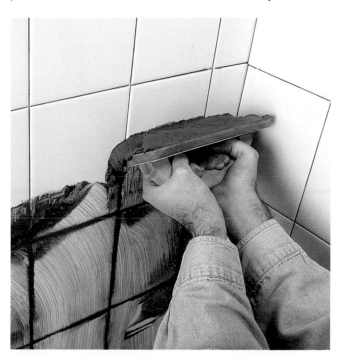

11 Once the mortar has cured on all of the tiles, which usually takes at least 24 hours, apply grout to the joints. Spread the grout using a rubber-faced float. Firmly force the grout into the joints, and remove the excess as you work. The more grout you remove now, the easier cleanup will be later.

INSTALLING A SOAP DISH

project

Although some soap dishes have a built-in bar (intended for a washcloth), they are not designed to withstand the weight of a person. It's wise to use dishes without a bar. You will find soap dishes that are sized to be used with standard-size tiles. When planning the project, install the field tiles, leaving an open space for the soap dish. Apply thinset to the wall and to the back of the dish.

TOOLS & MATERIALS

▎ Thinset mortar
▎ Small notched trowel
▎ Pointing trowel
▎ Soap dish
▎ Masking tape

1 Scrape off any dried adhesive residue from the full tiles surrounding the opening, and spread thinset adhesive on the wall.

2 Use a small trowel to butter the back of the soap dish with adhesive. Then press the dish into place, and align it with the adjacent tiles.

3 Maintain pressure on the dish as the adhesive sets by applying two long strips of masking tape across the front edge of the dish.

INSTALLING A RECESSED SOAP DISH

A RECESSED SOAP DISH is a convenient extra that you can build into your tile job. Some units require a small 2x4 frame to support the bottom and the sides of the dish within the wall. Use thinset adhesive to fasten a scrap piece of waterproof membrane to the inside of the framed support, overlapping the edge of the opening. Spread about ¼ inch of thinset adhesive on the back of the dish, and press it into place. The easiest option is to add a surface-mounted dish. It has a lip that rests on the surrounding tile. (See opposite.)

To mount a recessed soap dish, an extra piece of blocking is needed between studs. Plan for this before you begin installing tile.

INSTALLING A GRAB BAR

For maximum safety, don't rely on anchors in drywall or backer board. Fasten bar mounts directly to wall studs.

TOOLS & MATERIALS

▌ Power drill and masonry bit
▌ Anchors and screws ▌ Level
▌ Masking tape ▌ Screwdriver
▌ Grab bar

1 Locate wall studs, generally 16 in. on center. Apply masking tape to the surface of the tile, and drill using a masonry or glass-cutting bit.

2 You may not be able to hit a stud with every fastener. In such cases, use heavy-duty hollow-wall anchors or toggle bolts.

3 Tighten all fasteners until the bar does not move when force is applied to it. Be careful not to overtighten the screws and crack the tile.

MAKING A SHOWER SEAT

For maximum strength, fasten the seat directly into wall studs where possible.

TOOLS & MATERIALS

❙ Measuring tape and masking tape
❙ Power drill and masonry bit ❙ Anchors and screws ❙ Seat form and mortar mix
❙ Thinset adhesive and trowels ❙ Tiles
❙ Sponge float ❙ Caulk and caulking gun

1 Apply tape over the areas where you will need to attach the seat form. Then measure up from the shower pan to mark the attachment points.

4 Secure the hollow seat form with screws in the anchors. On new construction, you can add nailers between studs and drive screws without anchors.

5 Mix a batch of cement mortar to fill in the seat form. To provide a firm base without air pockets, use a trowel to work the mix into all corners.

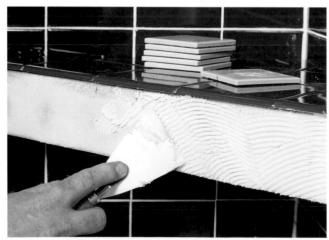

8 To avoid a grout seam along the seat edge, use tiles with a bullnose edge on top. The bullnose edges should cover the tiles on the seat face.

9 Set full tiles on the face of the seat, a contrasting color in this case. To keep them from sagging, you can add tape that laps onto the seat top.

2 Use a masonry bit in your drill to make holes for screw anchors. The tape helps to prevent chipping of the tile surface glaze.

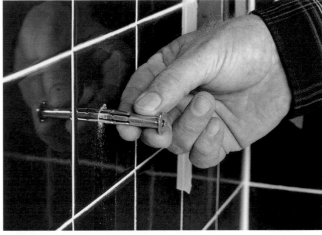

3 Remove the tape, and insert hollow-wall anchors into the holes. Match the drill bit diameter to the anchors so that they fit snugly.

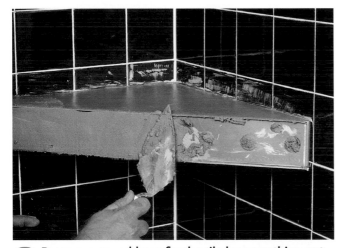

6 Prepare a sound base for the tile by smoothing out the mortar on the surface of the seat and spreading a thin layer on the front edge.

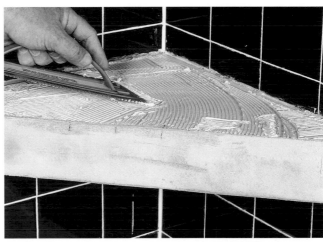

7 Once the mortar is dry, you can apply tile adhesive to the top and front of the seat. Cover the seat completely before raking out ribs of adhesive.

10 Use a sponge float to spread grout over the seat top and face. Work the mix back and forth at an angle to fill the seams.

11 Instead of grouting the seams along the walls, fill them with a flexible silicone caulk that can withstand slight flexing without cracking.

THINSET TUB ENCLOSURE

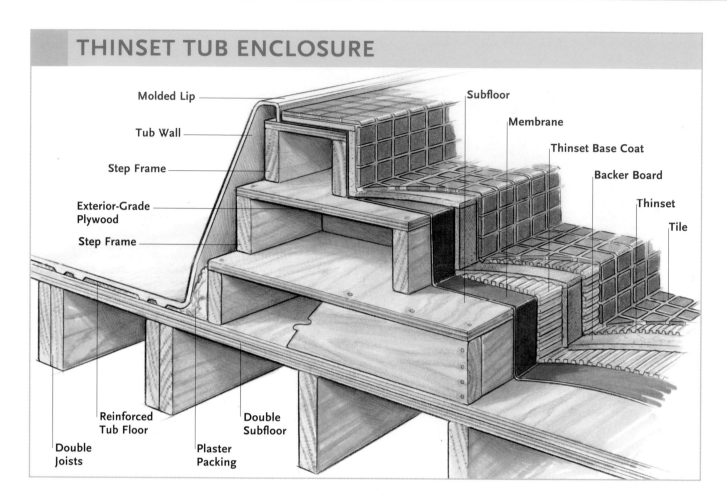

Molded Lip
Tub Wall
Step Frame
Exterior-Grade Plywood
Step Frame
Subfloor
Membrane
Thinset Base Coat
Backer Board
Thinset
Tile
Double Joists
Reinforced Tub Floor
Plaster Packing
Double Subfloor

FRAMING AND TILING TUBS

The easiest way to make a raised tub enclosure is to buy a drop-in tub and frame the platform around it. Tubs with a self-rimming lip overlap tiles on the top of the platform.

Floor Framing Support

In most cases you can rest the tub on the floor and build several steps into the side of your platform. Suspending a tub above the floor is possible but impractical and generally not necessary. For example, with tubs and whirlpool spas about 18 inches deep, you can build three steps, each with a comfortable 6-inch rise.

Because of the extra weight, however, it's wise to increase the strength of the floor. (Always check manufacturers' recommendations and local building codes, including requirements for approved grab bars or railings.) You can double up existing joists or add new joists spaced closer together than the standard layout of 16 inches on-center. Also plan on covering the existing subfloor with ¾-inch exterior-

grade plywood, glued and screwed in place. Many acrylic and fiberglass tubs have reinforcing ribs built into the base. But to make the most secure installation and guard against cracking the base finish, many professional installers set the tub base in a supporting bed of quick-setting plaster.

Platform Framing

When you plan the platform and steps, allow for structural framing, such as 2x6s, plus ¾-inch plywood topped with a layer of ½-inch cement-based backer board. Use slip-resistant tiles. On custom projects like this, it's wise to build the platform to suit the tile grid so that you can use full tiles.

When framing, you must allow for supply and drain lines, of course. It's also a good idea to include some kind of access panel or removable section so that you can reach the plumbing lines and make repairs easily.

Bear in mind that the platform should be at least as rigid as the floor. You may need to use pressure-treated joists set every 12 inches with joist hangers and corner hardware at the joints. Use screws instead of nails for more holding power.

THICKSET TILED TUB

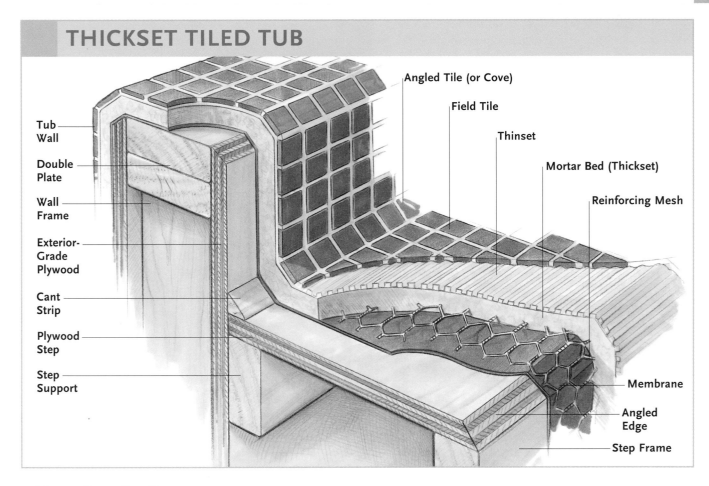

Tub Wall

Double Plate

Wall Frame

Exterior-Grade Plywood

Cant Strip

Plywood Step

Step Support

Angled Tile (or Cove)

Field Tile

Thinset

Mortar Bed (Thickset)

Reinforcing Mesh

Membrane

Angled Edge

Step Frame

Tiling the Platform

Once you have planned the layout for the best tile arrangement and established your working lines, tile the surfaces in the following order: step risers, step treads, platform surface, platform sides, and finally the walls surrounding the platform.

Bear in mind that if the tub is dropped in first, you will need to rout a rabbet around the edges of the tub cutout so that the rim sits flush with the rough platform surface. Then you'll need to tile over the rim with bullnose or quarter-round trim tiles. If the first course of field tiles around the trim tiles needs to be cut, the cut edges will be visible. Also, oval tubs and those with large radiused corners will require complicated cuts and irregularly shaped grout joints. Given these possible complications, consider a self-rimming tub with a raised lip that rests on top of the platform tiles.

If you are using cove trim tiles where the tub platform meets the walls, install these pieces before you set the full tiles on either surface. You might also use coves at the bottom of each riser, but this design requires careful planning when you frame the steps. Typically, you finish the

front edge of the step treads with bullnose tiles. You also can use special stair-nosing tiles for this purpose, if they are available.

Forming Custom Tubs

Tiled tubs can be virtually any shape or size you want. You can make square-edged enclosures or construct curved, free-form tubs covered with small ceramic mosaic tiles. But building such a tub is very difficult and best left to professionals.

The preferred method for building a tiled tub is to pour a reinforced concrete shell. A waterproof membrane is applied over the concrete shell, followed by a thickset mortar bed. Such a concrete tank requires a strong concrete footing set directly into the ground or exceptional framing that may need steel beams to provide enough strength. Also, the shell must be waterproof, and the floor should slope slightly toward the drain.

Another approach is to build a wooden form and apply a reinforced mortar bed over it. Such installations must be well reinforced, or movement in the wood substructure will crack the mortar bed and tile, causing leaks.

Tiling Tubs and Showers

Bead-board, below, combines with mosaic tiles for a sophisticated tub surround.

Mosaic glass tiles, right, create a colorful accent in this shower.

Painted tiles, below right, add color to a neutral background. Note the tiling around the window.

A corner tub surround, opposite top, creates a luxurious focal point in this bathroom.

Built-in seating, opposite bottom, makes any shower more useful and inviting.

design ideas

Large tiles, opposite, match the scale of the high ceilings in this bathroom.

Accent tiles, left, add distinction to the wall of this walk-in shower.

White wall tiles, above, are installed in a running-bond pattern.

The rustic charm of this log home, below left, is accentuated by the bright-blue tiles.

A simple color scheme, below, helps these different-shaped tiles work together.

design ideas

Stone tiles, below, cover a built-in tub surround.

Distinctive border tile, right, frames a tile wall.

A mosaic panel, bottom right, unifies floor and tub tile treatments.

Natural stone, opposite, creates a distinctive walk-in shower.

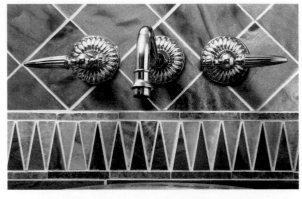

indoor projects 7

ALTHOUGH THE MOST COMMON TILE PROJECTS are floors, walls, and countertops, there are many other areas around the house where tile can provide an attractive surface that offers more durability and easier maintenance than many building materials. Some of the most popular are fireplace hearths and facings, woodstove surrounds, range hoods, and stairs.

Bear in mind that when you tile near any combustion source, such as a fireplace, you should check local building codes (and tile material data sheets) to be sure you are using fire-safe methods and materials.

TILING A FIREPLACE HEARTH

Whether you are building a new fireplace or remodeling an existing unit, you can use ceramic tile to make an elegant, fire-safe covering for the hearth. The width and depth of a new hearth may be established by local building codes, but most hearths extend at least 6 inches beyond the edge of the firebox on both sides and 16 to 24 inches from the front. This size should provide plenty of room to stack extra wood, an ash bucket, and some fireplace utensils.

TOOLS & MATERIALS

▌Framing square ▌Chalk-line box ▌Power drill and screws ▌½-inch cement-based backer board ▌Thinset and trowel ▌Tiles ▌Grout ▌Wood molding ▌Silicone caulk

1 Locate the center point of the firebox, and extend this into the room using a framing square. Generally hearths are at least 16 in. deep. Also, measure and mark the outlines of a backer-board base. The best thickness for this panel is ½ in. Thinner panels are too flexible, while thicker panels create a step that's easy to trip over.

SELECTING MATERIALS

MOST PEOPLE consider the selection of tile to be based mainly on personal taste. And while this is usually true, for hearth jobs the standards have to be higher. The selected tiles should be resistant to both heat from the firebox and impact from accidentally dropped logs. Heavy-duty quarry tiles, pavers, and glazed floor tiles are good choices, as are slate and other stone products. But to be sure your preference makes sense, discuss the issue with your tile supplier. They should know the products that can safely be used for your fireplace hearth. The same should be true of your local building department. As a general rule, if any product is offered in multiple thicknesses, choose the beefiest version.

If you are tiling over concrete, brick, or another masonry material, use nonflammable, heat-resistant mortar such as dry-set cement. Never use organic mastics. If you are tiling over a wood floor, like the plywood subfloor that we show above, install cement-based backer board that's at least ½ in. thick. If you have access to the joists below the hearth, take a few minutes to nail blocking between the joists to strengthen and stiffen the floor.

2 Spread thinset mortar on the floor, and lower the backer board into the mortar. Screw it to the floor in a 6–8-in. square pattern using corrosion-resistant screws made for backer board. Leave a ¼-in. gap between the backer board and the front of the firebox. This will be filled with silicone caulk after the tiles are installed.

3 Before applying any mortar, place dry tile on the backer board and double-check your layout to make sure it looks good. Mark clear installation lines on the panel; then spread thinset mortar over the surface using a notched trowel. Work in small areas so that the mortar doesn't cure before you cover it with tiles.

4 Carefully install the tiles in the mortar, maintaining consistent grout joints. Twist each tile back-and-forth slightly in the mortar to improve the bond. The cut tiles around the perimeter should be installed so that they are flush with the edges of the backer board.

5 After you have installed the tiles, wait at least 24 hours before applying grout to the joints. Wait another 24 hours. Then clean any grout haze from the tiles, and cut wood molding strips to fit around the backer board and tile. Apply caulk to the gap between the tiles and the firebox.

TILING A FIREPLACE SURROUND

The method you use to tile a fireplace surround will depend upon the circumstances. Generally, you can follow the same basic approach you use when tiling any interior wall. The main difference is that most installations require heat-resistant materials. Be sure to check your installation plans with your local building department to make sure everything you do complies with fire safety codes.

TOOLS & MATERIALS

▌ Level ▌ 1x2 or 1x3 pine stock for layout stick ▌ Tile spacers, thinset, and notched trowel ▌ Grout, float, and sponge
▌ Wood molding ▌ Stain and varnish
▌ Hammer, finishing nails, and nail set
▌ Caulk and caulking gun

1 One of the easiest and most reliable ways to plan a tile layout around a fireplace opening is to use a layout stick. Take a length of pine, and mark a series of full tiles (and grout joints) on the face. Move it from side-to-side and up-and-down to balance the layout and achieve the best appearance.

4 There are many different kinds of tile spacers available today. Probably the simplest and least expensive are the small plastic "plus signs" like this one. They are designed to fit between tiles, sit flat against the wall, and remain in place permanently. Once the mortar has cured, you can apply the grout over the spacers.

5 After the mortar has set overnight, you can usually fill the joints with grout the next day. Mix the dry grout with water until it has the recommended consistency; then spread it over the tile with a rubber-faced float. Once the grout has cured, wipe off the haze that's left behind using a damp sponge.

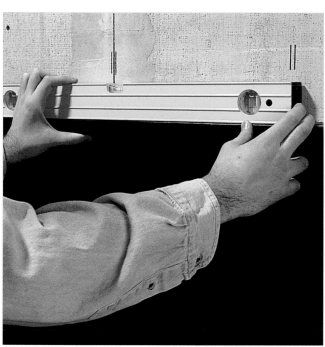

2 Check the top of the firebox opening using a level. If it is slightly out of level you may be able to correct the difference by altering the grout joints a bit. But if the opening is more than ¼ in. out of level, you should install the tiles maintaining consistent grout joints; and cut the tiles with a slight taper to fit along the firebox.

3 Spread thinset mortar on the substrate around the firebox using a notched trowel. Work in small areas that you can comfortably cover with tiles before the thinset starts to set. Rest the bottom tiles on the lip of the firebox, and maintain even grout joints using plastic spacers. Press the tiles firmly into the mortar.

6 The easiest way to make the transition from the tile facing to the surrounding wall is with wood molding. Cut this trim to fit; then apply stain (if desired) and a couple of coats of polyurethane varnish. Once the finish is dry, nail the trim to the wall using finishing nails; set the heads with a nail set; and cover them with wood filler.

7 Fill the space under the wall tile and behind the floor tile with silicone caulk. In most cases the clear type will look the best because it's not very noticeable. But white or black colored caulk may work better if they match (or come close to matching) the color of the grout or the firebox.

WOODSTOVES

Ceramic tile is a good choice for hearths and walls around woodstoves because it can withstand heat and sparks without shrinking, cracking, or charring the way wood does. But you should check local codes to be sure that your tile installation is fire-safe.

Basic Safety Considerations

Safety clearances can vary depending on the type of materials you have on the floor and wall—and on the type of stove you install. For example, stoves with a heat shield attached to the back generally can be much closer to walls than stoves without shields.

If you're installing a new stove, you almost certainly will need a building permit. The job can require structural alterations and an inspection even if you use prefab metal chimney sections. If you're tiling an existing installation, be sure that the old stove and flue are up to code.

Reducing Clearances to Tile

You can make a safe installation by keeping a stove 3 feet or more from the nearest wall. But most people don't want a stove sticking into the middle of a room. To prevent that, you can buy a stove with a heat-dissipating design. You can also make a tile installation on a false wall that creates an air baffle against the main house wall. With the right combination, you should be able to set a stove only 12 inches away from the wall.

Beneath the stove you normally have to install at least one layer of cement-based backer board. Walls often are more critical because stoves are designed to throw most of their heat through the sides and top. To cope with the heat, the most efficient wall consists of 1/2-inch noncombustible insulation board or 24-gauge sheet metal set 1 inch away from the house wall on noncombustible spacers. Most jurisdictions allow you to substitute backer board (a standard tile substrate) for the insulation board, but you should check to be sure.

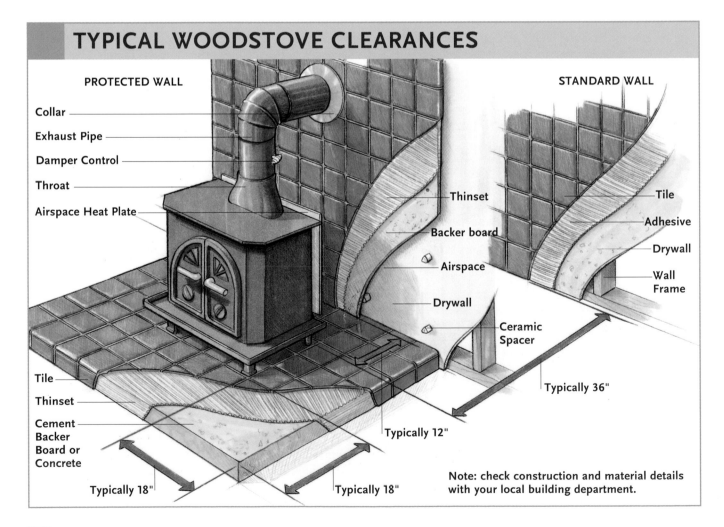

TYPICAL WOODSTOVE CLEARANCES

PROTECTED WALL

Collar
Exhaust Pipe
Damper Control
Throat
Airspace Heat Plate

Tile
Thinset
Cement Backer Board or Concrete

STANDARD WALL

Thinset
Backer board
Airspace
Drywall
Ceramic Spacer

Tile
Adhesive
Drywall
Wall Frame

Typically 36"
Typically 12"
Typically 18"
Typically 18"

Note: check construction and material details with your local building department.

TILING A SPACED WOOD-STOVE SURROUND

You can buy kits of ceramic spacers for spaced walls. Don't use wood blocks.

TOOLS & MATERIALS

▌Spacers and fasteners ▌Variable-speed drill ▌Cement-based backer board ▌Notched trowel and thinset ▌Grout tools and materials

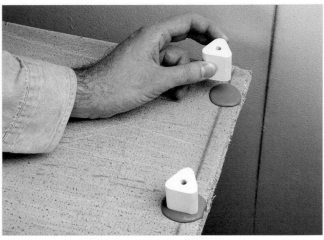

1 Attach spacers to the back of the backer board using thinset. Then use the spacer holes as guides to drill holes through the backer board.

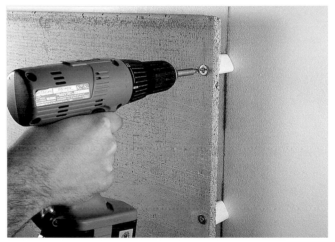

2 Secure the backer board by tightening a fastener that runs through the fireproof spacer into the house wall. The board should stand off 1 in.

3 Use a notched trowel to spread thinset over the backer board. The bed should be thick enough to bury the fastener and washer.

4 Set the main tiles in the pattern of your choice. Then trim the tiles that will surround the vent pipe using tile nippers.

5 Fit a metal trim ring around the vent pipe to cover open seams. This margin for error allows you to make rough cuts on the partial tiles.

RANGE HOODS

You can buy a range hood to tile or build a custom hood. But building one from scratch is quite a project for do-it-yourselfers because it's really several projects in one. You need to fabricate the hood structure and build-in wiring, a fan, a grease filter, a duct, and an exterior vent. It's often easier to add tile to a factory-made hood that can support tile.

Hood Tile

Where the tiles are concerned, you don't need extra thickness for impact resistance the way you do on a fireplace hearth. In fact, because of weight, thin glazed ceramic wall tiles are preferable. If the hood is curved, you can use ceramic-mosaic sheets.

Hood Dimensions

On a custom hood, plan ahead to avoid a lot of partial tiles and angled cuts. For example, you can design the hood apron to match the size of full tiles plus a grout joint. However, most range hoods slope inward from bottom to top, which means you'll have to use some wedge-shaped tiles.

Tiling a Hood

There are so many different range-hood designs that there is no one way to install the tile. But you should have good results following basic rules, such as using full tiles in a

You can use full tiles on an apron, and make angle cuts (allowing for grout joints or trim) on the sloping surfaces.

symmetrical pattern centered in the most visible area. If you need partial tiles (aside from angled tiles on the sloping edges), place them along the wall.

Apply adhesive according to the manufacturer's instructions with a notched trowel. You'll probably need to support the first row of tiles with a batten to prevent sagging. On hoods with finished edges below eye level, you can often trim the edge with bullnose tile. On higher installations and hoods with a thick edge, you should select tile that comes with matching radius-edge or other trim to conceal the substrate.

RANGE-HOOD MATERIALS

STOVE FIRES are among the most common types of house fires. They can start so easily and spread so rapidly that you should take care not to build a hood out of combustible materials that could add fuel to a blaze.

You may find that a building inspector will allow you to make a hood with wood framing as long as both sides are covered with fire-rated drywall. Or you may be able to cover the framing with cement-based backer board, which makes a good substrate for tile. Material selection may also be influenced by how far away from the range you locate the hood.

Steel Hoods. A sheet-metal company can fabricate a heavy-gauge steel hood that will support tile. After rough-

ening the steel surface with sandpaper, you set the tiles with an epoxy adhesive or with a latex-cement thinset mortar with additives that bond to steel. Some are rated to resist temperatures over 300°F, which is a lot hotter than a range hood will get during normal operation.

Wooden Hoods. You can build a plywood-covered wood frame and install drywall or backer board over the structure. If codes permit, this may be the best choice if you have an unusual installation or plan to use an unusual combination of tile sizes.

Prefab Hoods. The thin sheet metal generally used for these hoods is too flexible to support the weight of the tile without cracking the grout joints.

TILING A RANGE HOOD

Create a frame for the tile out of hardwood trim or special trim tiles.

TOOLS & MATERIALS

▌Wood (and wood sealer) or tile trim
▌Camps, finishing nails, hammer
▌Cement-based backer board ▌Drill and fasteners ▌Wood sealer, brush ▌Notched trowel and thinset ▌Tile ▌Grout materials

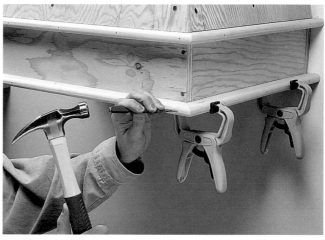

1 Frame the apron with hardwood trim applied with glue and finishing nails. You can also use tile trim over cement-based backer board.

2 Once the wood trim is secured, you can apply panels of cement-based backer board to the apron and sloping faces of the hood above.

3 To protect the wood trim as you tile, apply a protective coat of sealer. This makes it easier to wipe away traces of thinset and grout.

4 A series of mosaic-like tiles are used on this project to focus attention on the apron. No spacers are needed because the tiles have spacer lugs.

5 Set full tiles in a ribbed bed of thinset on each sloping face of the hood. Where the fields meet, you can use wood trim, tile trim, or a grout joint.

STAIRS

It is possible to tile both stair treads—the part you step on—and stair risers—the vertical panel between treads. But it can be difficult for do-it-yourselfers to match the design of wood steps and create an overhang at each tread. The more doable and often better looking project is to use tile on the risers only as a decorative feature, and stick with traditional wood planks with an overhang on the treads.

If you want to tile the treads, consider ordering special stair-tread tiles that come with a rounded nosing to project slightly past the front edge of the riser.

Another option is to use large, unglazed quarry or paver tiles that are often used for the treads on outdoor steps. You may be able to create a small tread overhang with tile and supporting trim strips. You can't project a standard floor tile past the riser without support because it is too likely to crack.

Whatever tile you select for the treads should be slip-resistant and durable enough to withstand heavy foot traffic. Tiles for risers, on the other hand, can be relatively thin glazed wall tiles. You can install them in a continuous band across the riser or add just one accent tile in the center of the riser.

You can combine heavy-duty tread tiles that have a built-in nosing with thinner, more decorative tiles on the risers.

DESIGN CONSIDERATIONS

MOST STAIRS are strong enough to support tile because they are designed to support people. But some treads do flex slightly, which is just enough to disrupt tile grout and lead to repair problems and possible safety hazards. It's difficult to detect minimal flexing, although the sound of squeaking wood is a sure sign that stair components are moving. On an existing staircase with this problem, you can take several approaches.

The most drastic improvement is to add a center stringer. This effectively cuts the span of each tread and riser in half, providing twice as much support. But you can also screw steel angle brackets to treads and risers, insert wooden wedges, and add long wood screws to create a more secure connection between the stairs and supporting walls. Another option is to install wooden blocks with glue and screws along the seams between treads and risers at midspan where they are weakest and most likely to flex.

Of course, it's possible to make these improvements only if you have access to the stair framing from below or if you remove a tread. But if you are planning to cover treads and risers with tile, you can drive screws through exposed surfaces to tighten up the structure. If you do this, it's wise to countersink the holes so that screwheads are flush and cannot crack the tiles.

If you are tiling over concrete steps (a project that is more likely outside than inside), clean the masonry surfaces to improve adhesion, and repair any cracks or other faults that could create weak spots under the tile. If you are building a new set of wooden steps for tiling, provide a suitable substrate such as exterior-grade ¾-inch plywood. On deep treads you can use two layers of the plywood to prevent flexing as long as you stay within code limits for riser and tread dimensions. You can also guard against cracking by using a flexible caulk along the seam between tread tiles and riser tiles.

TILING STAIRS

Set riser tiles on temporary spacers or nails to hold them in place.

TOOLS & MATERIALS

▌Screwdriver and fasteners ▌Hardware, or wood blocks and glue ▌Sander and medium-grit sandpaper ▌Trowel and adhesive ▌Caulk and caulking gun

1 You can strengthen stairs with closed framing by driving screws at an angle through the face of the riser and into the tread.

2 To improve the adhesive bond on risers, scrape off old paint, and sand down any rough spots using medium-grit paper.

3 Use a small notched spreader to cover the riser with adhesive. Do a test fit with full tiles ahead of time to plan any partial cuts.

4 Snip off the bottom of a spacer so that you can insert it between the tile and the tread. You can also use finishing nails to keep the tile from sagging.

5 Once the tile has set, grout the vertical seams, and wipe away the final grout haze. Use flexible caulk in the tread seams.

design ideas

Natural stone tiles, opposite, give an under- stated look to this fireplace.

Tiled stair risers, left, add a distinctive touch to this home.

An exhaust-hood border, above, ties the area into the rest of the design.

A large fireplace area, below, relies on tile for a cohesive design.

design ideas

A tile surround, above, becomes a focal point in this room.

Colorful tiles, below, are used as a surround for a rotisserie.

Unusual shapes, right, add interest to this fireplace and hearth.

Terra-cotta tiles, opposite, complement the cabinetry in this room.

design ideas

Marble treads and ceramic-tile risers, below, create a distinctive stairway.

Terra-cotta pavers, right, serve as a backdrop for painted tiles that resemble a throw rug.

A band of bright tiles, below right, add a touch of color to this range hood.

Mosaic glass tiles, opposite, add sparkle to a fireplace wall.

outdoor projects 8

CERAMIC AND STONE TILES are among the most elegant surfacing materials you can use for a patio, walk, or entryway. The type of tile you choose may be determined by the weather in your region. In warm, relatively dry regions, for example, soft-bodied, nonvitreous pavers are often used. These include low-fired, handmade Mexican pavers and cement-based Saltillo tiles. Both types are porous and will not hold up in wet or cold climates. In most areas of the country, you will need a hard-bodied vitreous or impervious tile, such as porcelain pavers or quarry tiles. In cold climates, select tile and grout that resist freezing temperatures.

PREPARING CONCRETE FOR TILE

project

There is a wide variety of exterior tiles that can be installed over an existing concrete slab. Preparing a slab for tiles is a relatively straight-forward job, as shown in the photos here. The only specialized tool that you are likely to need is a power grinder. These tools are similar to right-angle drills. But they are outfitted with an abrasive disk instead of a drill bit, and they operate at much higher rpms. They are typical rental items.

TOOLS & MATERIALS

▐ Framing square or level ▐ Power grinder (or hammer and cold chisel) ▐ Broom and mop ▐ Patching mortar and mason's trowel ▐ Hose ▐ Scrub brush and detergent

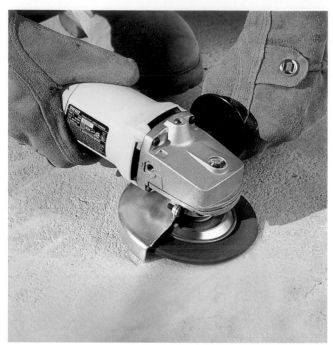

1 Slide a straightedge, such as a framing square or a long level, over the surface of the slab to check for any high spots. Mark these; then grind them flush with the surrounding surface using a power grinder. You can also use a hammer and a cold chisel. These tools will do the job, but they will also take much longer.

TILING OVER CONCRETE

IF YOU'RE STARTING FROM SCRATCH, you can pour a solid slab to support the tile. If you have a solid slab already, you'll generally only need to do a little cleaning and touch-up work. But you can also use tile to cover up surface cracks and other problems in an older patio, and let the existing masonry serve as a foundation.

If the slab is badly fractured, however, you may have to pour new concrete footings and refinish the surface. It's a lot of work, but it makes sense when compared with paying someone to break up the old patio and cart it away. If, on the other hand, the slab is covered with surface cracks but is still flat and stable, it is a good candidate for pouring a thin cover slab.

If parts of the slab are tilting in different directions and bobbing up and down each season like slow moving icebergs, you'll have to beef up the slab's support system. It's best to consult an engineer or an experienced masonry contractor about this work. Unfortu-

nately, you can't get good results if you try to patch major cracks on a slab that moves seasonally. The cracks are bound to open again and break the grout joints, the tiles, or both after the first cold winter.

2 Sweep away any debris left behind from grinding off the high spots. Then rinse the surface using a garden hose. You could also use a high-pressure power washer, which can deliver hundreds of pounds of pressure per square inch. These tools can remove dust, mildew, and even stubborn stains.

3 Once the surface and the cracks are free of debris, let them dry; then fill the cracks with patching mortar. Mix the powder according to the package directions. Spread the mortar over the crack; then force it in with the trowel's point. Finish up by smoothing the area with the bottom of the trowel.

4 After the mortar in the cracks has cured, wash the entire surface using a heavy-duty concrete cleaner and a brush. This will remove any grease, wax, or other contaminants that would undermine the bond of the tile to the slab. On a large job, this step can take quite a bit of time, but the results are well worth the effort.

5 It may be important to wash the slab to clean away any contaminants from the surface. But it's just as important to rinse away the concrete cleaner when you are done. A garden hose can do the job, but if you have a pressure washer, use it instead. It cleans better because it can force water into the smallest crevices.

BUILDING A NEW CONCRETE BASE

To build a tiled patio or walk, you'll need a solid concrete slab. To build one, you'll probably need a permit and a plan that shows its location and construction details.

A typical slab has several layers that combine to strengthen the concrete. To reduce stress, they should rest on undisturbed or compacted soil. This helps to prevent settling that can cause cracks. In cold regions, you generally have to build a perimeter foundation for the slab that extends below the frost line. That may require extra excavation and other work that may be beyond the capabilities of do-it-yourselfers.

The bottom layer of a sturdy, code-approved slab usually consists of several inches of compacted gravel. You pour the concrete on top of it. To strengthen the pour, you need to embed a layer of welded wire. This is the home version of large-scale rebars that you see on larger construction projects. To provide maximum strength, try to set the flattened welded wire (it comes in a roll) in the bottom third of the pour. To do this, you can use pieces of brick or specialty supports called "chairs" to suspend the wire as you pour the concrete.

On large slabs, you'll also need one or more control joints. These slices in the slab surface (you see them every few feet in concrete sidewalks) control minor cracking.

If the patio joins the house, you'll also need an isolation joint so that the structures don't move against each other. To make one before pouring the concrete, temporarily insert a strip of wood to create about a ⅜-inch gap between the concrete and the foundation. When the pour sets, fill the space with backer rod and caulk.

Lastly, plan the slab to account for even multiples of the tiles you plan to use. Also account for the grout joints. If you're building from scratch, you can eliminate the need for partial tiles.

PATIO SLAB CONSTRUCTION

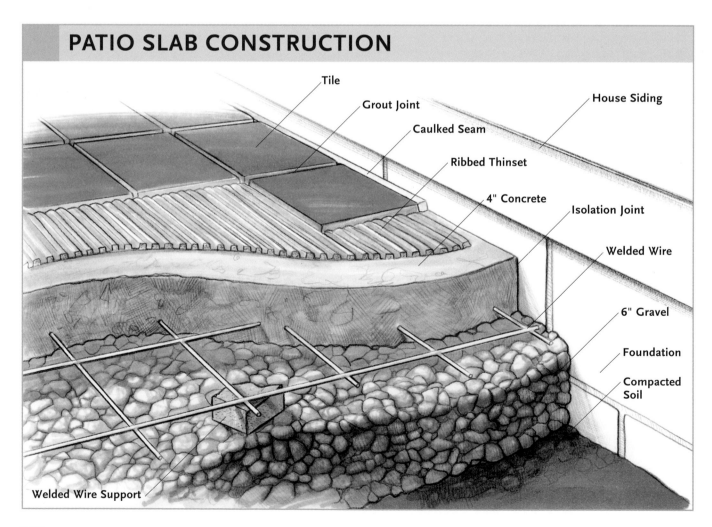

Tile · Grout Joint · Caulked Seam · Ribbed Thinset · 4" Concrete · House Siding · Isolation Joint · Welded Wire · 6" Gravel · Foundation · Compacted Soil · Welded Wire Support

In small outdoor spaces, left, use one size and color of tile to make the area seem larger.

In a large outdoor space, above, you can use contrasting tile colors to define separate areas.

CUTTING A CONTROL JOINT

IT MAY SEEM STRANGE to slice up the surface of a slab and cut what amounts to big, straight cracks on purpose. But each shallow groove acts as a kind of magnet that collects minor cracking where you can't see it. You can cut these joints with a masonry saw after the concrete hardens or use a jointing trowel against a straightedge guide while the mix is still wet.

Cut control joints using a masonry blade once the concrete hardens. You can also cut them in wet concrete with a special trowel.

MAKING SLAB FORMS

project

To calculate the amount of concrete you will need, multiply the length times the width times the average depth of the forms to yield a cubic-foot total. Divide this number by 27 to arrive at the number of cubic yards you'll need. On small projects you can mix the concrete yourself in a wheelbarrow, which holds about 3 cubic feet. But for more than a yard of concrete, order it from a ready-mix company.

TOOLS & MATERIALS

▌ Wood for batter boards, stakes, and forms
▌ Shovel and sledgehammer ▌ Hammer and clamps ▌ Level, mason's string, and drill ▌ Snips, welded wire, and wire supports
▌ Trowel and concrete installation tools
▌ Concrete ▌ Wheelbarrow

1 Install batter boards and stakes at the corners of the slab layout to support the layout strings that show the boundaries of the forms. Make sure that these strings are square or parallel with each other and that they are level. The strings are also used to indicate where excavating is required to accommodate the forms.

4 Use welded wire to reinforce the concrete. This material is generally sold in large rolls and is cut to fit with tin snips or lineman's pliers. Once the wire is cut, flatten it out by rolling it loosely in the opposite direction. The wire should fit easily between the form boards so that it doesn't get hung up on the forms during the pour.

5 Install the wire so that it will be in the middle of the slab. This is accomplished by supporting it on small sections of brick. Slide the bricks under the points where the wire sections join—every 12 to 16 in. Be careful when pouring the concrete. Make sure the wire isn't pushed off these bricks.

2 Begin building the forms by cutting 2x4 stakes, with a point on one end, and driving them into the ground around the perimeter of the area. Make sure that they go in straight. If these stakes are tipped in any direction, they will distort the forms by making them bow in or out.

3 After the stakes are in place, install the form boards by clamping them to the sides of the stakes. Tighten the clamps securely; then check the top of the form for level. Adjust up and down as necessary. Once satisfied, attach the forms to the stakes by driving screws through the stakes and into the back sides of the form boards.

6 Fill the forms with mixed concrete carried to the site in wheelbarrows. As the forms fill, slide a trowel along the sides between the form boards and the new concrete. This helps to eliminate voids in the concrete against the form, which will result in smoother sides that are stronger and look better.

7 Smooth the surface of the concrete using a straight 2x4 that bridges the distance between one side of the form and the other. Use a gentle side-to-side sawing motion, and make sure all sections of the surface are filled with material before you move on to the next section. Keep the top of the form free of debris.

LAYING TILES ON A SLAB

Once your concrete is poured and the surface is finished, you're still not ready for tiling. This is a gradual process. The hardening process that supplies the strength and durability of concrete should take place in a damp environment. If the concrete dries out too quickly, it can lose strength. You must keep the finished surface damp for at least a couple of days; a full week is better. Just mist the surface with a garden hose three or four times a day.

TOOLS & MATERIALS

▌ Measuring tape and chalk-line box
▌ Thinset mortar and notched trowel
▌ Tiles and spacers ▌ Grout and grout float
▌ Straightedge

1 Trial layouts are important on any tile job, including those on an exterior slab. As always, you want to keep the partial tiles balanced and as large as possible because small tiles at the perimeter look bad. This job contains a couple of support posts, which should fall on a grout joint.

4 When all the layout lines are marked, cut the notch on the other tile that surrounds the support post, and check it for fit. When satisfied, remove the tiles; sweep the surface clean; and spread enough thinset to cover 10 to 12 sq. ft., working in small sections to give you enough time to install the tile before the mortar sets.

5 When you reach sections where no cutting is required, you can apply mortar over a larger area. Spread the thinset uniformly with a notched trowel; then press the tiles in the mortar. Use tile spacers to maintain even grout joints, and check for square periodically using a framing square.

2 A preliminary dry layout will reveal any complications. It was easy to make the posts fall on tile seams. But it wasn't easy to center the post in the seam. We settled on a good compromise of notching the first post tile to the right size and placing it against the post.

3 Using the notched tile as the starting point of the layout, snap chalk lines to lay out the rest of the project. You can use the same approach you use for tiling floors. Try to accommodate full tiles across the slab.

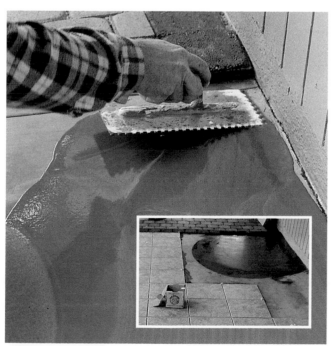

6 If you encounter an unexpected problem when you're installing the tile, such as the low spot shown here, stop tiling; remove any thinset from the problem area; and make the repair. In this case, a thin slurry of self-leveling concrete patch solved the problem. Let the patch dry (inset) before laying the tile.

7 After all the tiles are installed and the thinset has cured, usually for at least 24 hours, mix up some grout, and spread it into the joints using a rubber-faced float. Work with firm, diagonal strokes to make sure you force the grout to the bottom of every joint. Wipe away any excess grout as you work.

193

TILING ENTRY STEPS

To tile over a set of concrete steps or a landing, follow the same basic procedures used on patios. But there are a few wrinkles to this project.

First of all, you need to consider safety. That means allowing for a code-approved handrail on steps and staying within approved limits on stair treads and risers. You can check these with the local building department, but generally the rise should be no less than 4 inches and no greater than 7¾ inches. Treads typically must be at least 3 feet wide and about 10 inches deep. If old steps don't meet code, make the necessary improvements. This may include removing an old handrail and installing a new one through the tile. You should also have an isolation joint between the steps and the house foundation so that the two structures don't work against each other.

Tile the Steps

You can use the same tiles on steps that you use on patios. Remember to mention to the supplier that the tiles will be used outside so that you get vitreous tile, which prevents water penetration.

Lay out the steps carefully, particularly if you are tiling both treads and risers. If you are adding tiles to the risers, for example, you need to take their thickness into account when you plan the treads. Generally, the riser tile thickness is covered with a bullnose tile on the tread. Plan on making a test layout.

PREPARING DAMAGED STEPS FOR TILE

Be careful nailing into concrete. The material is so hard that nails can snap; be sure to wear gloves and safety glasses.

TOOLS & MATERIALS

▌Wire brush ▌Wood for forms ▌Concrete nails and hammer ▌Trowel and patching mortar ▌Work gloves and safety glasses

1 Wire-brush the damaged area to remove any loose material. To contain the patch material, extend the faces of the step with plywood.

2 To help the patch adhere, you can coat the step with a concrete bonding agent. It also helps to set a few concrete nails about halfway in.

3 Trowel on fresh patching mortar to fill up the cavity. Work the trowel along the insides of the forms to create smooth edges without voids.

TILING A POOL DECK

Confine your efforts to the deck area and let a pool contractor install the coping and do any tile work in the pool. Then you can go to town with borders and patterns of tile basically the same way you would on a patio.

But no matter what type of inground pool you have, you can install an isolation joint and tile to its structural boundary. Start by compacting the dirt adjacent to the pool coping.

Follow up with standard slab construction, including a base of 6 inches of gravel and 4 inches of poured concrete reinforced with welded wire. When you build forms for the pool-surround, build in the same kind of slope (about ¼ inch or so per linear foot) that's used on patios. Slope the surround away from the pool on all sides. Locate the outer perimeter of the surround a few inches above grade to prevent water-washed soil and other contaminants from flowing into the pool.

Contrasting tiles help to define boundaries that make the area around a pool more attractive and safe.

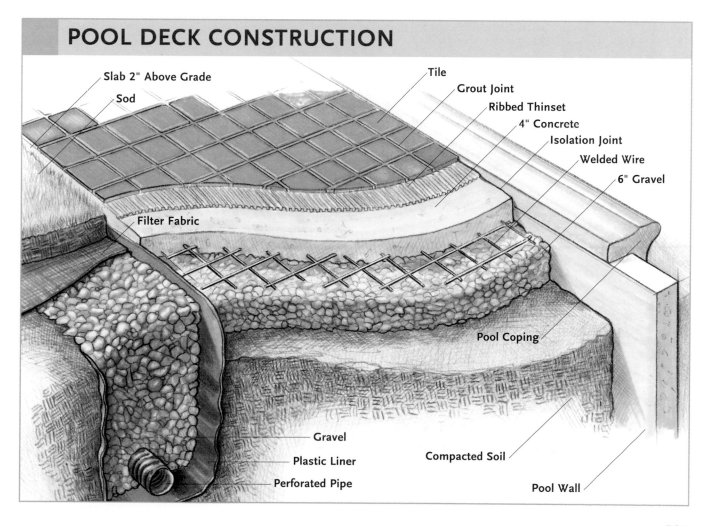

POOL DECK CONSTRUCTION

Slab 2" Above Grade
Sod
Tile
Grout Joint
Ribbed Thinset
4" Concrete
Isolation Joint
Welded Wire
6" Gravel
Filter Fabric
Pool Coping
Gravel
Plastic Liner
Perforated Pipe
Compacted Soil
Pool Wall

Porcelain tiles, above, are a good choice for pool and fountain decoration.

Colorful tiles, below, draw attention to this small water garden.

A combination of natural stone and tile, above right, creates a distinctive garden fountain.

Tiled steps, bottom right, call attention to this curving outdoor stairway.

Terra-cotta pavers, opposite, are a favorite floor covering for outdoor living areas.

design ideas

Two types of tile, opposite, form a distinctive border for a curved driveway.

A tile detail, left, is a distinctive way to display a house address.

An outdoor kitchen, below left, benefits from the natural weather-resistance of tile.

Ceramic tile, below right, serves as a floor for a front porch.

Tile stars, bottom, as the main attraction in a home's water feature.

design ideas

Using varying sizes of natural stone, right, adds a great deal of design interest to the area.

Slate tiles, below, are a favorite material for patios and walks.

Marble tiles, opposite, help set off this covered outdoor living area.

repairs and maintenance 9

CERAMIC AND STONE TILES provide durable and easy-to-clean surfaces. But tiles do need occasional maintenance and sometimes repairs. Grout is often the weak link in a tile installation. It generally attracts mildew and discolors more easily than tile. Grout is also more likely than tile to crack from minor structural settling and other everyday stresses in the building frame. When a tile joint opens in a wet area, you can't afford to put off repairs. An open grout joint allows water to seep in and work under the tile. That can break the adhesive bond and begin to rot the supporting structure. And as layers of the plywood weaken and separate, they're likely to cause more cracks.

ROUTINE CLEANING

For day-to-day cleaning, simply wipe down tile with warm water and a sponge. On floors, regular sweeping or vacuuming should prevent dirt and grit from scratching the tile surface and grinding into grout joints.

There are many proprietary tile cleaners that can remove light buildups of dirt, grease, soap scum, and water spots. For stubborn stains, try a strong solution of soap-free, all-purpose cleaner or a commercial tile cleaner. Don't use acid-based cleaners; they can attack grout. Always rinse thoroughly with clean water. Unglazed tiles should be resealed after cleaning.

If you really need to scour the surface, use a woven-plastic pot scrubber rather than steel wool, which sheds flecks of metal that leave rust stains in grout joints. Avoid using soap-based detergents because they generally dull the tile surface. Remember not to mix different types of cleaners, and never mix ammonia with bleach or products that contain it. That combination can produce lethal fumes.

Removing Common Stains

Strong solutions of all-purpose cleaners or commercial tile cleaners will remove most stains. (Find suggestions for removing some of the more unusual stains in "Removing Stains," right.) But in most households there are two common cleaning problems: mold on tile grout, and a buildup of soap scum that's sometimes combined with hard-water scale.

To clean grout joints, first rinse the area with water. Then use a toothbrush dipped in household bleach to remove stains. Stubborn stains may respond to a preliminary dose of straight bleach. If the grout is colored, test a spot to make sure the bleach will not cause discoloration. If it does, use a commercial tub-and-tile cleaner. Use household bleach with caution: wear rubber gloves and safety glasses.

Another option is to try a combination of household bleach and an abrasive cleanser (one that does not contain ammonia). Make a paste, scrub it on, and rinse. If some spots remain, cover them with a wet mound of the paste for several hours before scrubbing again. To tackle a stain that is deep in the grout, try a soupy poultice of baking soda and liquid detergent mounded up and left on the spot overnight to draw out the stain. Don't try to grind away blemishes with abrasives that can cut into the tile glaze.

To remove mild soap deposits and hard-water spots, spray the surfaces with an all-purpose, nonabrasive cleaner, and let it soak in for a few minutes before rinsing. If some deposits remain, mist the area with vinegar, and let it sit for a few minutes before wiping. If all else fails try a proprietary soap-scum or mineral-deposit remover.

Hard-Water Problems

If you are concerned mainly with mineral deposits in water that form white scale, check into the problem yourself with a water-hardness test kit, or try this simple home test. Add ten drops of liquid detergent to half a glass of tap water, cover, and shake. If the detergent forms high, foamy suds, you have relatively soft water and probably don't need water-conditioning equipment. If the detergent forms low, curdled suds, you have relatively hard water and probably could benefit from a water-softening system.

REMOVING STAINS

STAIN	REMOVAL AGENT
Grease & fats	Household cleaners
Tar, asphalt, oil, grease, oil paints, petroleum-based products	**Indoors:** Charcoal lighter fluid; then household cleaner, water rinse **Outdoors:** Concrete cleaner
Ink, mustard, blood, lipstick, merthiolate, coffee, tea, fruit juices, colored dyes	**Mild:** 3% hydrogen peroxide **Deep:** Household bleach
Nail polish	**Wet:** Charcoal lighter fluid **Dry:** Nail polish remover
Liquid medicines, shellac	Denatured alcohol
Rust	Rust remover; then household cleaner; rinse
Chewing gum	Chill with ice wrapped in cloth; scrape off surface

Caution: some cleaning agents are toxic, caustic, or flammable. Use only as directed by the manufacturer and with adequate protective gear.

BASIC CLEANING

Unglazed tiles may take several hours to dry after a wet cleaning and look blotchy until they do.

TOOLS & MATERIALS

▮ Vacuum cleaner or broom ▮ Cleanser
▮ Bucket ▮ Scrub brush and sponge
▮ Roller and tile sealer ▮ Rubber gloves

1 Sweep or vacuum a tile floor before scrubbing with a cleanser to avoid grinding surface dust and grit into the tile glaze.

2 Although there are many specialized tile cleaners and stain removers, a mild solution of cleanser and water handles general cleanup.

3 Use a scrub brush with soft bristles on stubborn stains. If you use bleach on tough stains, wear rubber gloves and safety glasses.

4 Rinse the floor after cleaning to remove any cleanser residue. Regularly wring out the sponge and change the rinse water.

5 You can apply a sealer over a dry, clean floor of unglazed tiles. This helps to protect both the tile and the grout joints.

ROUTINE MAINTENANCE

Sealing Grout and Unglazed Tile

You can apply a clear sealer to the grout joints only, or to the entire floor, if you have unglazed tiles. A sealer doesn't eliminate cleaning and repairs, but it does add a measure of protection against stains. You may find that some sealers darken the tile a bit in the same way that a clear coating can slightly change the hue of brick or concrete in a patio.

The drawback is that you need to reapply the sealer about every two years (or as specified by the manufacturer) to maintain protection.

A combination of wall and floor tile can provide an easy-to-clean, low-maintenance environment.

CLEANING OLD GROUT

Remember that straight bleach may discolor the surface of unglazed tile. You should test a small section to see the result.

TOOLS & MATERIALS

- Household bleach ▪ Scrub brush
- Grout sealer ▪ Applicator or artist's brush
- Rubber gloves and safety glasses

1 Few specialized cleaners can match the effectiveness of straight household bleach on mold-stained grout. Test a small section on dark grout.

2 Let a puddle of bleach sit for a few minutes on the most stubborn stains. Brushing can help to dislodge deep stains in porous grout.

3 Once the grout is clean and dry, reduce further staining (and cleaning) by coating grout seams with a clear sealer.

Optional Waxing

Many tile waxes and buffing compounds are available for unglazed tile floors. Some are colored to enhance the appearance of unglazed terra-cotta tiles or pavers. After cleaning the floor with a soap-free floor cleaner and rinsing thoroughly with clear water, let the surface dry, and buff out the existing wax to restore the shine. When it's time to reapply wax, you'll need to strip off any old wax, wash the floor with a mild detergent, and rinse thoroughly with clear water. Two or three light coats of wax look better than one heavy coat.

The drawback is that a buffed wax finish can make tile floors slippery. You have to decide whether the improved appearance and protection is worth the increased risk of an accidental slip or fall.

Maintaining Tub Surrounds

If you spill water on a tile counter or floor, you'll probably wipe it up. But the tile and grout around tubs and showers get soaked and stay wet regularly. This makes the area difficult to keep clean and a prime candidate for a complete overhaul.

Often the most troublesome location is the seam between the wall tiles and the edges of the tub. One reason for trouble: some do-it-yourselfers grout this seam along with the rest of the tile joints instead of filling it with caulk. A liberal bead of flexible silicone caulk helps to shed water. It also bridges the gap between the wall tiles, which are subject to one set of stresses, and the tub, which is subject to another.

REMOVING OLD GROUT

Be sure to adjust the guide so that the cutting bit does not dig into the sides of the tiles.

TOOLS & MATERIALS
▌ Rotary power tool and grout-removal attachment
▌ Grout saw (optional)

1 Grout-removal attachments are typically sold as accessories for rotary-type power tools. The guide hood clamps over the chuck.

2 The hood of the attachment seats the tool on the tile, while guide nibs keep the cutter aligned with the grout seam.

3 With a grout-removal attachment, you can clean out the seams between tiles without damaging or dislodging the surrounding tiles.

Repairs and Maintenance

Once the grout is cleaned (or replaced), taking the time to seal it will greatly reduce the need for more cleaning.

TOOLS & MATERIALS

▮ Tile cleaner and applicator ▮ Hook scraper and razor cutter ▮ Grout mix, rubber float, squeegee, rag, and sponge ▮ Sealer, caulk, and caulking gun

1 To scrape out damaged or deeply stained grout you can use a carpet knife, a small grout saw, or a power grout-removal tool. (See page 207.)

4 When the damaged grout is cleared and the joints are brushed clean, mix fresh grout to a workable, slightly soupy consistency.

5 Spread grout with strokes on the diagonal to the seams. Use a rubber-surfaced float for spreading and a squeegee for removing the excess.

8 To smooth out a bead of caulk, the not-very-high-tech tool that often works best is the end of your finger dipped in soapy water.

9 To prevent water from seeping behind the plumbing fixtures and under the tiles, also apply a thin bead of caulk around the fixture edges.

2 On many older installations you need to slice off one or more layers of old caulk and clean out the seam between the tile and the tub.

3 If you need to scrub stubborn soap scum or water deposits, use a sponge or plastic pad, not steel wool, which can cause rust stains.

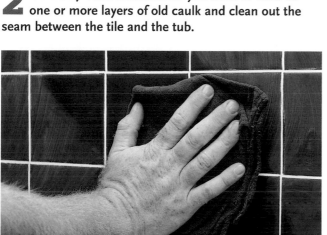

6 When the grout sets up you can make the first of many passes with a clean, damp rag to remove extra residue and the final grout haze.

7 To create a waterproof seal between the bottom row of tiles and the tub, apply a continuous bead of a flexible, silicone-based caulk.

10 This grout calls for wet curing. You keep it damp by misting with water several times a day. Plastic sheets help contain the moisture.

11 To protect the new grout and reduce the need for future maintenance and repairs, seal the seams with clear silicone sealer.

FIXING BROKEN TILES

project

You can break a damaged tile into small pieces that are easy to remove, but the reverberating forces of a hammer and cold chisel are likely to cause even more damage to surrounding tiles because the grout locks one to the next. A better approach is to first remove the grout. To do this job, a grout saw is indispensable. It is easy to use, but removal can take quite a while. When you are working on a finished wall, take your time and try to minimize the shock to surrounding areas.

TOOLS & MATERIALS

▌Drill and masonry bit ▌Grout saw
▌Cold chisel ▌Wood chisel or scraper
▌Thinset mortar and notched trowel

1 Start the job by drilling small holes through the grout at the corners of the tile using a masonry bit. These holes provide points for the grout saw to grip, and they prevent damage to the grout joints around adjacent tiles. You can also drill holes through the cracked areas of the tile to make it easier to chip out smaller pieces.

3 Once the grout is removed, it's easy to chip out the pieces of tile. You can use a cold chisel or a stiff scraper blade for this job. But one of the best tools is a dull wood chisel. The thin edge of the blade slides easily under the tile; then you just pry up gently to free the tile from the mortar underneath.

4 After all of the tile pieces and surrounding grout are removed, you need to scrape away any mortar adhesive that's still left on the wall. Again, a dull wood chisel is a good tool for this job. It's sharp enough to get under the mortar but not so sharp that it will dig into the wall. A sharp putty knife can do a similar job.

2 You can also loosen the grout around a tile by scraping it out with a sharp utility knife. But a grout saw is a much more efficient tool to use. The cutting edge of this tool is covered with bits of very hard abrasive, usually diamond particles, and it's wider than a utility knife blade.

5 When the wall surface is free of mortar, grout, and dust, mix some thinset mortar, and spread it on the wall using the end of a notched trowel. If you have trouble getting a uniform bed of thinset on the wall, spread some on the back of the tile to make sure to get a good bond.

DIGGING OUT GROUT

YOU CAN DIG OUT GROUT with a small cold chisel, or you can remove it with a power grout-removal tool. (See how it works on page 207.) But two easier and less-expensive alternatives are to use a simple grout saw or a series of masonry drill bits. The grout saw is a lightweight tool that has a very sharp blade covered with durable abrasive. The tool works like any other saw, just push it back and forth. Because the grout is so hard, this job will take a while. But it's a low-impact tool that won't cause damage to any surrounding tile. Another low-impact approach is to use a drill and masonry bits. Select a bit diameter that matches the width of the grout joint and simply drive a series of overlapping holes along the grout joints. The best approach is to use both tools. Start with the drill bit to loosen the grout, then use a grout saw to remove the waste.

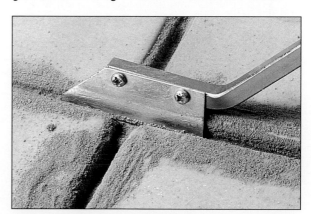

Hand grout saws have both abrasive and toothed cutting blades.

Masonry bits have an extended carbide tip to cut through grout.

Repairs and Maintenance

FIXING TRAPPED TILES

project

Tiles that crack in the middle of the floor are easy enough to replace. But the job becomes more difficult when part of the tile is trapped beneath a cabinet, sink, toilet, or other fixture that you can't or don't want to remove. Trapped tile repairs can be tricky. But it's possible to make a repair that will look as though you replaced the entire tile.

TOOLS & MATERIALS

▮ Drill and masonry bit ▮ Cold chisel or flat-blade screwdriver ▮ Rotary tool and cutting wheel ▮ Glass cutter ▮ Compass scriber or contour gauge ▮ Wet saw or snap cutter and tile nippers ▮ Thinset mortar and notched trowel ▮ Silicone caulk and caulking gun

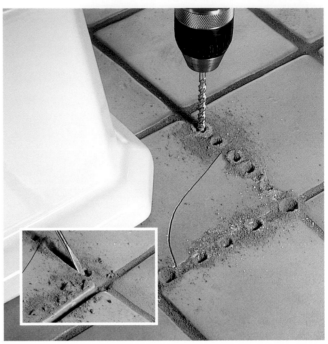

1 Drill release holes around the damaged tile using a masonry bit. Space the holes about ½ inch apart. Then remove the grout with a flat-blade screwdriver (inset) and a sharp utility knife. When all the broken grout is removed, vacuum up the dust and debris so that it won't damage other tiles.

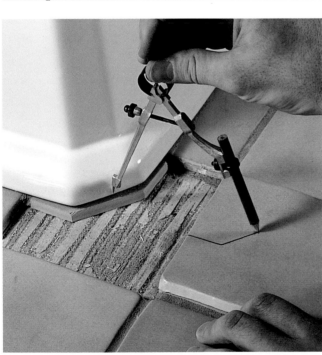

4 Removing the old tile isn't difficult. But shaping a replacement tile requires a great deal of accuracy. This starts by using a compass scriber to mark a full tile to fit the opening, Place the replacement tile directly over one of the adjacent tiles, and trace the shape of the obstruction on the surface.

5 The best way to make a complicated cut like this is with a tile wet saw. Renting these common tools is inexpensive and makes good sense if you have a lot of cuts. You can also use a snap cutter and tile nippers. The job will take longer, but by working carefully you should get good results.

2 Use a rotary tool with an abrasive cutting wheel to cut the trapped part of the tile. If you hold it firmly, work slowly, and don't bend the abrasive wheel as it cuts, it will grind through the tile easily and leave a smooth surface behind. For best results, score the cut first, and go back and finish cutting in sections.

3 Once the rotary tool has cut through the tile, chip out the damaged section using a flat-blade screwdriver or a dull wood chisel. If hand pressure isn't enough, strike the head of the screwdriver with a hammer. For best results, work the blade under the edge of the tile; then pry up gently until the tile breaks.

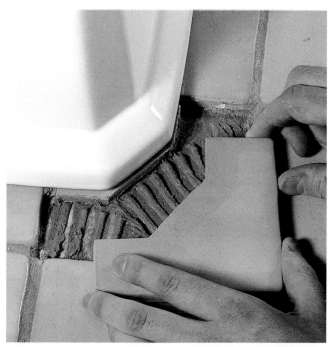

6 Remove the old mortar from the floor, and vacuum up the remaining dust and debris. Then spread new thinset mortar using a notched trowel. Lower the replacement tile into the mortar, and twist it slightly to make sure it seats completely. Then use tile spacers to maintain uniform grout joints.

7 Mix up a small batch of tile grout, and fill the joints as required. Let the grout dry; then seal the joint between the new tile and the obstruction with silicone caulk. Apply a healthy bead, especially in damp or wet areas. If the bead is rough, you can smooth it right after it's applied using a wet finger.

APPENDIX

tile installation specs

JUST AS THERE are hundreds of uses for tile, there are an equal number of ways to install it. Unfortunately, not all of them are correct, and some can lead to cracked tiles and damage to whatever is beneath the tile, such as a countertop or the framing in the floors or walls. Installation specifications based on research from the Tile Council of North America will help you do the job right. You will find some basic installations here. For more information, go to www.tileusa.com.

TILE FLOORS OVER CONCRETE SLABS

A PROPERLY INSTALLED CONCRETE SLAB, whether outside or in, is a durable high-quality structure that can yield many years of service with little or no problems. Durable, yes; but attractive, well...

It's fair to say that not everyone thinks concrete is beautiful. And because of this, many different strategies for covering up all the slabs in our life have been developed. Certainly two of the most popular, in both the commercial and residential worlds, are carpet and tile.

Carpet is usually the choice where a softer, more forgiving surface is desired. But carpet requires a lot of routine maintenance, and it wears out. A good tile installation, on the other hand, can last indefinitely and only needs a little soap and water when it gets dirty.

There are nearly as many ways to install tile over a concrete slab as there are baseball teams in the major leagues. This book has previously explained the most common techniques. But to provide some sense of the variety of installation methods, we've included five additional approaches shown here.

Drawing #1 shows ceramic tile over an exterior slab. This traditional approach includes a 1¼-in.-thick bed of mortar on top of the slab and an optional waterproof membrane over the mortar. This is a job better suited to a contractor than a homeowner. Proper installation of a thick mortar bed can be difficult.

Drawing #2 shows the same exterior slab with the optional waterproof membrane. But in this case, the tile is bonded to the concrete with an easy-to-install thinset (either dry-set or latex) mortar.

Drawings #3 and **#4** show the companion installations for interior concrete slabs. The first features the thick mortar bed, while the second uses thinset or latex mortar to set the tile. Both approaches omit the optional waterproof membrane shown in **#1** and **#2**.

Drawing #5 is identical to **#4,** but it features an organic adhesive instead of a thinset mortar. The organic adhesive is easier to use, and it dries by evaporation (which is quicker) instead of curing, as is the case with mortar.

Appendix: Tile Installation Specs

1. EXTERIOR TILE FLOOR ON MORTAR BED OVER CONCRETE SLAB

2. EXTERIOR TILE FLOOR ON CONCRETE SLAB

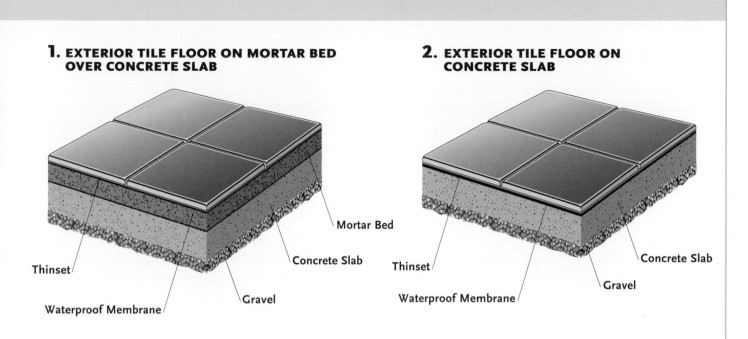

Mortar Bed

Concrete Slab

Thinset

Gravel

Waterproof Membrane

Concrete Slab

Thinset

Gravel

Waterproof Membrane

3. INTERIOR TILE FLOOR ON MORTAR BED OVER CONCRETE SLAB

4. INTERIOR TILE FLOOR ON CONCRETE SLAB

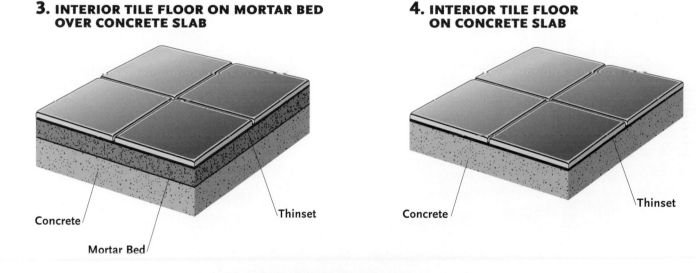

Concrete

Thinset

Mortar Bed

Concrete

Thinset

5. INTERIOR TILE FLOOR IN ADHESIVE ON CONCRETE SLAB

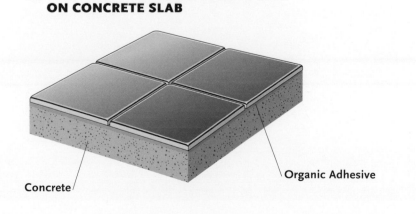

Concrete

Organic Adhesive

217

TILE FLOORS OVER WOOD SUBFLOORS

IN MOST HOUSES, a wood subfloor forms the base material for nearly all ceramic floor-tile installations. These include the big three: kitchen, bathroom, and powder room floors. But tile is also the default floor finish for foyers, mudrooms, and pantries. The biggest difference between a concrete and a wood subfloor is stability. The concrete, at least in interior installations, is very stable. Wood (usually plywood) is less stable. The tile installation specs take this into account, as you can see in the drawings here.

Drawing **#1** shows the tile in a substantial mortar bed reinforced with metal lath. The reinforcement and the weight of this mortar bed make it very stable. In **Drawing #2** you see a much easier installation. To install the tile, all that's needed is organic adhesive. But to stabilize the floor you must have a double layer of ⅝-in.-thick exterior-grade plywood.

You can achieve the stability of the double layers of plywood by substituting a cementitious backer board for the top underlayment layer of plywood as shown in **Drawing #3.** When properly installed, the backer board provides better water resistance and is therefore a good choice for wet areas.

For damp areas, some tile contractors substitute the cementitious backer board in **#3** with a water-resistant gypsum backer board shown in **Drawing #4.** This material is for indoor use only and for areas that are occasionally damp, not frequently wet.

One of the best alternatives to a mortar-bed base is shown in **Drawing #5.** Instead of using extra plywood or backer boards for a stable base, this installation features a poured gypsum underlayment. This material is installed as a thick liquid and is nearly self-leveling. Once it's dry you have a very smooth, uniform base.

Appendix: Tile Installation Specs

1. INTERIOR TILE FLOOR ON MORTAR BED OVER WOOD SUBFLOOR

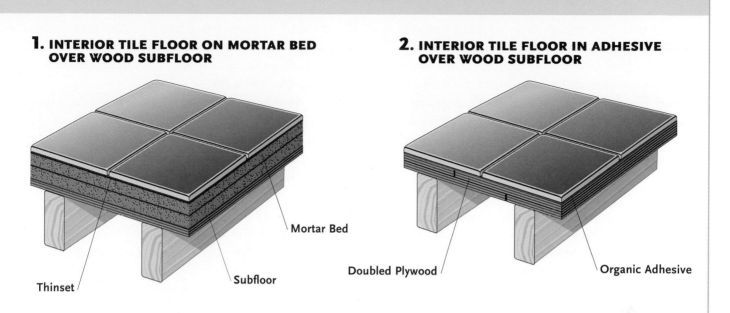

Mortar Bed

Subfloor

Thinset

2. INTERIOR TILE FLOOR IN ADHESIVE OVER WOOD SUBFLOOR

Doubled Plywood

Organic Adhesive

3. INTERIOR TILE FLOOR ON CEMENTITIOUS BACKER BOARD OVER WOOD SUBFLOOR

Cementitious Backer Board

Thinset

Plywood

4. INTERIOR TILE FLOOR ON GYPSUM BACKER BOARD OVER WOOD SUBFLOOR

Gypsum Backer Board

Thinset

5. INTERIOR TILE FLOOR ON POURED GYPSUM OVER WOOD SUBFLOOR

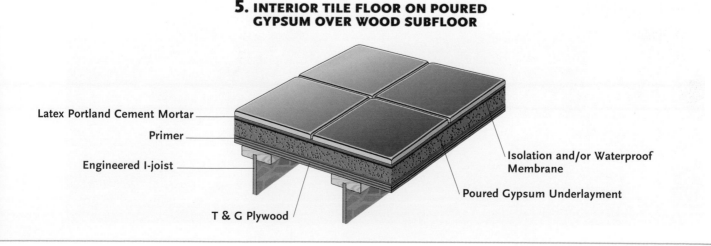

Latex Portland Cement Mortar

Primer

Engineered I-joist

Isolation and/or Waterproof Membrane

Poured Gypsum Underlayment

T & G Plywood

Appendix: Tile Installation Specs

TILE FLOORS OVER RADIANT HEAT

OVER THE LAST 20 YEARS, in-floor radiant heat has grown from a niche heating system to one that's practically ubiquitous. There are several good reasons why it's nice to have radiant heat around. It warms rooms evenly; it doesn't need a loud blower to push air through a tangled system of ducts; and it keeps your feet toasty whether you're in the bathroom, the living room, or the basement.

Radiant heat has made tile floors more popular and forced the development of new installation specs to keep things running right. Five of these approaches are shown here. The first deals with a hydronic (hot water) radiant system. The other four feature electric-resistance radiant heat.

Hydronic in-floor heat is the traditional approach that's been around for decades. As you can see in **Drawing #1,** the tile installation is pretty simple. Pouring a concrete slab around the tubing is another matter. In **Drawing #2** the installation of the electric radiant heat is a little easier: it's embedded in mortar over a standard slab. Once the mortar is cured, the tile job is very straightforward.

When the radiant heat goes over a wood subfloor instead of a concrete slab, installation options start expanding. In **Drawing #3** you see electric radiant components surrounded by a poured gypsum underlayment. The gypsum provides a beautiful, flat surface for installing the tile.

In **Drawing #4** the heating components are embedded in latex mortar over a double layer of plywood subfloor. The EGP designation on the mortar stands for "exterior-glue plywood," which means that the mortar has an additive that makes it bond very well to the plywood subfloor.

Drawing #5 shows nearly the same approach as **#4.** But in this case, a cementitious backer board takes the place of the underlayment layer of subfloor plywood. The tile is installed the same way in both cases.

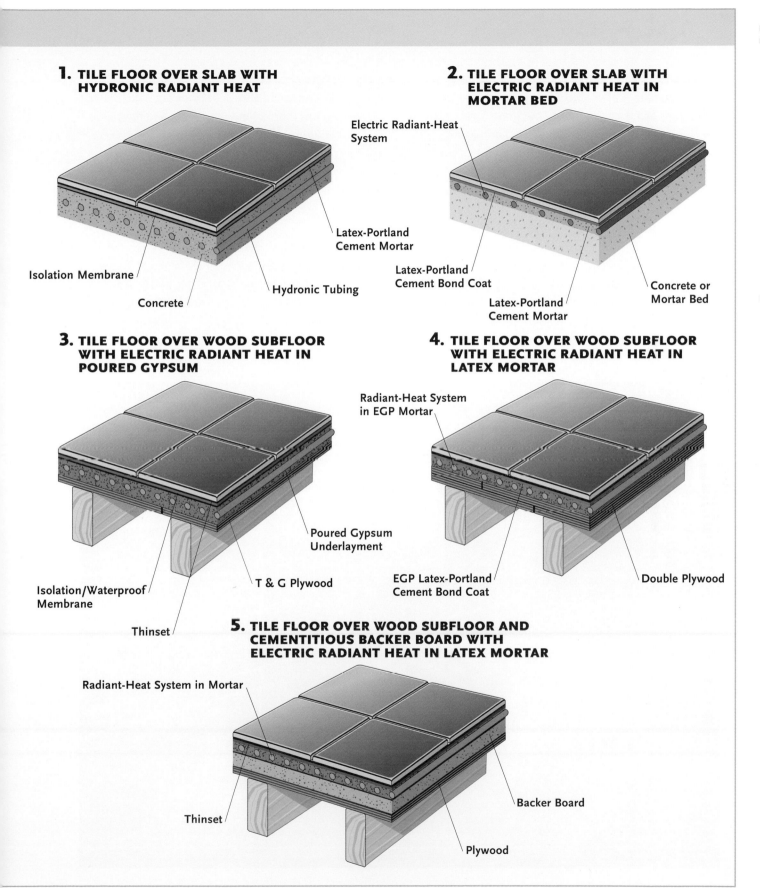

1. TILE FLOOR OVER SLAB WITH HYDRONIC RADIANT HEAT

Isolation Membrane

Latex-Portland Cement Mortar

Concrete

Hydronic Tubing

2. TILE FLOOR OVER SLAB WITH ELECTRIC RADIANT HEAT IN MORTAR BED

Electric Radiant-Heat System

Latex-Portland Cement Bond Coat

Latex-Portland Cement Mortar

Concrete or Mortar Bed

3. TILE FLOOR OVER WOOD SUBFLOOR WITH ELECTRIC RADIANT HEAT IN POURED GYPSUM

Poured Gypsum Underlayment

Isolation/Waterproof Membrane

T & G Plywood

Thinset

4. TILE FLOOR OVER WOOD SUBFLOOR WITH ELECTRIC RADIANT HEAT IN LATEX MORTAR

Radiant-Heat System in EGP Mortar

EGP Latex-Portland Cement Bond Coat

Double Plywood

5. TILE FLOOR OVER WOOD SUBFLOOR AND CEMENTITIOUS BACKER BOARD WITH ELECTRIC RADIANT HEAT IN LATEX MORTAR

Radiant-Heat System in Mortar

Thinset

Backer Board

Plywood

Appendix: Tile Installation Specs

TILE WALLS

GENERALLY SPEAKING, tile walls are not exposed to the same amount of abuse that tile floors suffer. This happy fact is sponsored by our good friend gravity. None of us walks on a wall, at least not all day long. And water never pools on a wall and then tries to attack the mortar or adhesive underneath that holds everything together. Because of this, you might think that tiling a wall would be easier than working on a floor. Unfortunately, most of the time it's not, because the same gravity that keeps weight and water off a wall wants to pull the wall into a pile of debris on the floor.

A quick look at **Drawing #1** will show you that things haven't gotten much easier. A typical exterior masonry wall must first be covered with a mortar bed that's reinforced with metal lath. Only when this bed is cured can the tile be attached with thinset mortar. If

an exterior masonry wall is sound and very flat you can use the easier method shown in **Drawing #2.** This just calls for thinset mortar between the tile and the wall.

Another approach is shown in **Drawing #3.** Here, an interior masonry wall that has a rough, uneven surface must be tiled. The best choice is to apply a smooth mortar bed over the wall surface. When this is cured, the tile can be installed with thinset mortar or adhesive.

Drawings #4 and **#5** show two good ways to tile over walls built with wood or metal studs. In **#4** gypsum board is specified as the base and in **#5** a cementitious backer board is installed. The gypsum method is only appropriate for dry conditions. But if an optional waterproof membrane is added to the backerboard installation, it can be used in wet or dry areas.

1. EXTERIOR TILE WALL ON MORTAR BED OVER MASONRY WALL

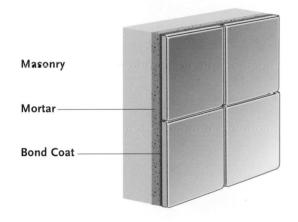

Masonry Wall

Metal Lath

Scratch Coat

Mortar Bed

Bond Coat

2. EXTERIOR TILE WALL ON LATEX MORTAR BED OVER MASONRY WALL

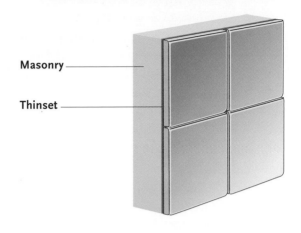

Masonry

Thinset

3. INTERIOR TILE WALL ON MORTAR BED OVER MASONRY WALL

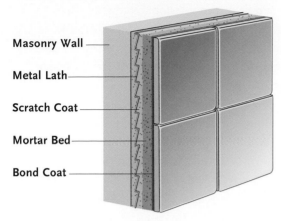

Masonry

Mortar

Bond Coat

4. INTERIOR TILE WALL ON GYPSUM BOARD OVER WOOD OR METAL STUDS

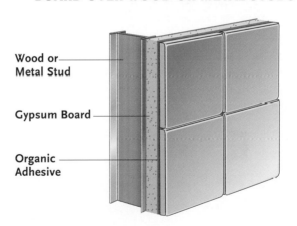

Wood or Metal Stud

Gypsum Board

Organic Adhesive

5. INTERIOR TILE WALL ON WATER-RESISTANT BACKER BOARD OVER WOOD OR METAL STUDS

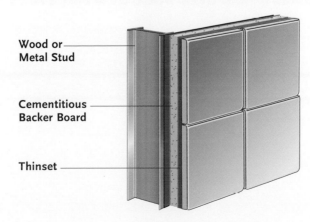

Wood or Metal Stud

Cementitious Backer Board

Thinset

Appendix: Tile Installation Specs

TILE CEILINGS, TUB AND SHOWER WALLS, COUNTERTOPS,

A CEILING may not be the first place that most of us install tile, but commercial installations have used tile ceilings forever. Just think about the gym shower rooms when you were a kid. One of the most common approaches is shown in **Drawing #1**. The wood framing is simply covered with gypsum board, and the tile is attached with adhesive or thinset mortar.

Tiling the walls above bathtubs and shower stalls is another common tile job. **Drawings #2** and **#3** show the typical approaches: **#2** calls for a base of water-resistant gypsum board, while **#3** features a cementitious backer-board base. In both cases, the bottom course of tile does not rest on the lip of the tub or shower unit. Space is left for flexible sealant (caulk) between the materials.

Kitchen and bath countertops are two more places where tile is very popular. Several sections in this book feature different countertop treatments. The methods shown in **Drawing #4** are practically the default choices for most jobs. The countertop is made of plywood that's covered with a membrane, followed by backer board, thinset mortar, and tile.

A great way to update old, or slightly damaged, tile without making a lot of mess is to cover the old tile directly with new tile. This process is usually called a tile-over-tile renovation. The four drawings shown here, **#5A, #5B, #5C,** and **#5D,** indicate four different approaches. In each case, the new tile is bonded to the old with thinset mortar or adhesive.

1. TILE CEILING OVER GYPSUM BOARD ON WOOD OR METAL FRAMING

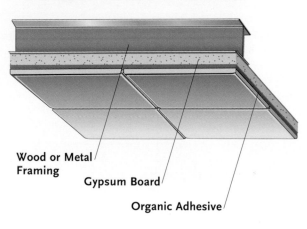

Wood or Metal Framing

Gypsum Board

Organic Adhesive

2. TILE BATHTUB WALL OVER WATER-RESISTANT GYPSUM ON WOOD OR METAL STUDS

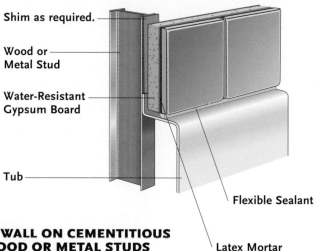

Shim as required.

Wood or Metal Stud

Water-Resistant Gypsum Board

Tub

Flexible Sealant

Latex Mortar

3. TILE BATHTUB/SHOWER WALL ON CEMENTITIOUS BACKER BOARD OVER WOOD OR METAL STUDS

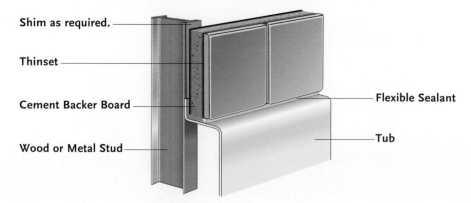

Shim as required.

Thinset

Cement Backer Board

Wood or Metal Stud

Flexible Sealant

Tub

AND TILE-OVER-TILE RENOVATIONS

4. TILE COUNTERTOP OVER CEMENTITIOUS BACKER BOARD ON PLYWOOD BASE

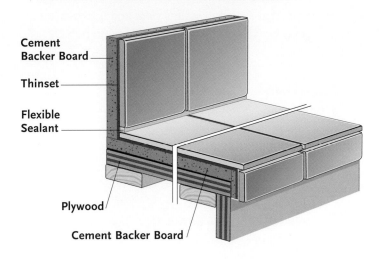

Cement
Backer Board

Thinset

Flexible
Sealant

Plywood

Cement Backer Board

5A. NEW TILE WALL OVER OLD TILE WALL

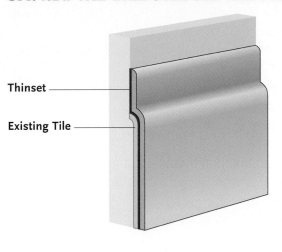

Thinset

Existing Tile

5B. NEW TILE WALL OVER OLD TILE WALL

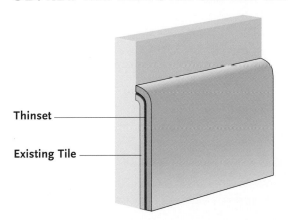

Thinset

Existing Tile

5C. NEW TILE WALL OVER OLD TILE WALL

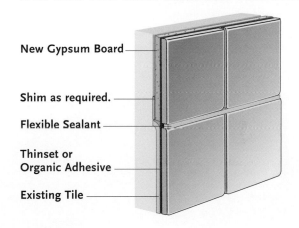

New Gypsum Board

Shim as required.

Flexible Sealant

Thinset or
Organic Adhesive

Existing Tile

5D. NEW TILE WALL OVER OLD TILE WALL

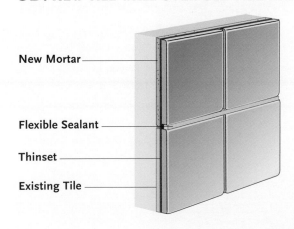

New Mortar

Flexible Sealant

Thinset

Existing Tile

This list of manufacturers and associations is meant to be a general guide to additional industry and product-related sources. It is not intended as a listing of products and manufacturers represented by the photographs in this book.

American Marazzi
359 Clay Rd.
Sunnyvale, TX 75182
972-226-0110
www.marazzitile.com
American Marazzi manufactures an extensive line of floor and wall tile.

American Olean
888-268-8453
www.aotile.com
American Olean manufactures ceramic tile for floors, walls, and countertops. The company's Web site features a number of design tools.

American Slate Company
611 Industrial Ave.
Boynton Beach, FL 33426
800-258-6245
www.americanslate.com
American Slate Company offers slate and quartzite tiles for floors, roofs, walls, fireplaces, and countertops.

Bosch Tools
877-267-2499
www.boschtools.com
Bosch manufactures power tools, including corded and cordless drills, sanders, saws, and other specialty tools.

Ceramic Tile Institute of America, Inc.
12061 W. Jefferson Blvd.
Culver City, CA 90230
310-574-7800
www.ctioa.org
The Ceramic Tile Institute of America supports the expanded use of ceramic tile and is a good source of information about tiling.

Craftsman Tools
Sears
800-349-4358
www.craftsman.com
Craftsman sells more tools than any other retailer. Through an extensive chain of outlets, Craftsman offers a wide variety of basic tools and tile specialty tools.

Crossville, Inc.
P.O. Box 1168
Crossville, TN 38557
931-484-2110
www.crossvilleinc.com
Crossville, Inc., manufactures an expansive selection of residential tile in a variety of styles, colors, and sizes.

Custom Building Products

13001 Seal Beach Blvd.
Seal Beach, CA 90740
800-272-8786
www.custombuildingproducts.com
Custom Building Products offers an extensive line of construction materials and tools, including thinset mortar mix, organic mastic, grout, and grout sealers.

Daltile

7834 C. F. Hawn Frwy.
Dallas, TX 75217
214-398-1411
www.daltile.com
Daltile offers an inventory of ceramic tile for kitchens, baths, and entryways, as well as for outdoor applications, such as pools and spas.

Deutsche Steinzeug America, Inc.

367 Curie Dr.
Alpaharetta, GA 30005
770-442-5500
www.dsa-ceramics.com
Deutsche Steinzeug America, Inc., manufactures tiles coated with Hydrotect, a protective finish that, according to the company, guarantees brilliant cleanliness with a minimum of cleaning effort.

Fraser Clay Works, Inc.

64 Myrtlewood Dr.
Mountain Home, AR 72653
870-492-5031
www.fraserclayworks.com
Fraser specializes in high-relief hand-crafted wall tiles.

Hitachi Power Tools

www.hitachipowertools.com
Hitachi manufactures innovative power tools, including cordless drills, pneumatics, and special tools for concrete and masonry.

Hyde Manufacturing Company

54 Eastford Rd.
Southbridge, MA 01550
800-872-4933
www.hydetools.com
Hyde makes a wide variety of hand tools for masonry and drywall, and tools for setting and finishing tile, such as spackle blades and floats for applying grout.

Makita Industrial Power Tools

14930 Northern St.
La Mirada, CA 90638
800-462-5482
www.makita.com
Makita manufactures power tools, including a full line of cordless drills.

Motawi TileWorks
170 Enterprise Dr.
Ann Arbor, MI 48103
734-213-0017
www.motawi.com
Motawi manufactures decorative tile in assorted sizes and shapes.

National Association of the Remodeling Industry (NARI)
P.O. Box 4250
Des Plaines, IL 60016
847-298-9200
www.remodeltoday.com
This organization represents thousands of home improvement professionals and offers consumers links to NARI-certified local contractors.

National Concrete Masonry Association
13750 Sunrise Valley Dr.
Herndon, VA 20171
703-713-1900
www.ncma.org
This trade group, representing the concrete masonry industry, offers a variety of technical information, design aids, and publications.

National Kitchen & Bath Association
687 Willow Grove St.
Hackettstown, NJ 07840
800-843-6522
www.nkba.org
This national organization supplies design and planning information for kitchen and bath projects and referrals to professionals.

Q.E.P. Co., Inc.
1001 Broken Sound Pkwy., NW, Ste. A
Boca Raton, FL 33487
561-994-5550
www.qep.com
Q.E.P. Co., Inc., manufactures a broad line of flooring-related tools for both DIY and professional installers. These include trowels, floats, wet saws, and snap cutters.

National Fire Protection Association
1 Batterymarch Park
Quincy, MA 02169
617-770-3000
www.nfpa.org
This national group provides a wide variety of information on fire-safe construction.

The Noble Company
P.O. Box 350
Grand Haven, MI 49417
231-799-8000
www.noblecompany.com
The company manufacturers CPE flexible membrane material, which is used to waterproof tile installations in showers and tubs.

Porter-Cable Tools
4825 Hwy. 45 N.
Jackson, TN 38305
731-660-9354
www.porter-cable.com
This tool company produces a variety of corded and cordless drills, saws, sanders, and specialty tools.

Ryobi Tools
800-525-2579
www.ryobitools.com
Ryobi features an extensive line of power tools for every home-improvement project.

TEC Specialty Products, Inc.
H.B. Fuller Construction Products Inc.
1105 S. Frontenac Rd.
Aurora, IL 60504
800-832-9002
www.tecspecialty.com
TEC Specialty Products supplies a wide range of flooring adhesives and surface-preparation products, including mortar, grout, and joint sealants.

Tile Council of America, Inc.
100 Clemson Research Blvd.
Anderson, SC 29625
864-646-8453
www.tileusa.com
This trade group represents hundreds of tile companies and offers a variety of information on tile, including the Handbook for Ceramic Tile Installation.

U.S. Gypsum Corp.
550 W. Adams St.
Chicago, IL 60661
800-950-3839
www.usg.com
U.S. Gypsum supplies gypsum-based products, including drywall, joint compound, backer board, and other tile installation and substrate products.

Zircon Corporation
1580 Dell Ave.
Campbell, CA 95008
800-245-9265
www.zircon.com
Zircon manufactures electronic hand tools, including measuring tools, laser levels, and stud sensors.

Glossary

Apron tile Tile set along the face of a structure—for example, along the front of a countertop edge or the vertical border of a sloping kitchen range hood.

Backer board Cement-based sheet material used as a substrate for tile on walls, floors, and counters. The material of choice in any wet area, such as a kitchen or bathroom, because it is unaffected by water. Also called cementitious backer units, or CBUs.

Backer-board cutting tool A carbide-tipped hand tool used to score cement-based backer board so that it can be snapped to the proper size.

Backsplash The vertical surface at the back of a countertop.

Bedding block A block of wood (usually a 2×4) wrapped in carpeting or other padding used to level a high tile with the tiles around it.

Bridging Supports attached between joists to increase rigidity of a floor. You can purchase steel bridging or make your own from common dimensional lumber.

Bullnose tile A trim tile with at least one rounded-over edge used to finish outside corners.

Buttering Applying adhesive with a trowel to the back of a tile to supplement the adhesive spread on the setting bed or substrate.

Caulk One of many flexible compounds used to fill gaps between construction materials. Some key tile joints are filled with caulk instead of grout.

Cement-bodied tile Tiles made of mortar instead of clay, generally providing the appearance of stone or pavers without a surface glaze.

Chalk-line box A long string wound in a box filled with colored chalk used to mark straight layout lines by snapping against floors or walls.

Contour gauge A tool used for duplicating complex shapes, such as moldings, onto tile, which then can be cut to fit.

Control joint A shallow groove cut into the surface of a concrete slab before it hardens to confine small stress cracks. Minor cracks form down in the grooves instead of in the slab surface.

Course One horizontal row of tiles or other materials.

Cove tile A shaped trim tile with a slightly curved base that creates a rounded joint between adjacent walls, a wall and a floor, or other surfaces that meet at right angles. Often used as a sanitary detail along the bottom of bathroom walls.

CPE Chlorinated polyethylene membrane, a flexible, rubbery sheet commonly used instead of lead or other materials to waterproof the floor of a tile shower or tub.

Curing The period of time that concrete, tile adhesive, or grout must be left in order for it to reach its working strength. Curing time is usually longer than drying time.

Expansion joint A space left between two surfaces that allows for natural expansion and contraction, typically filled with a flexible backer rod covered with caulk.

Field tile A full-size tile in the main area of the installation.

Float A long-handled tool used to smooth a concrete surface. More generally with tile, a term describing the process of shaping and smoothing a bed of mortar with a trowel.

Floated bed A bed of mortar, often with a slope or other irregular shape, that serves as the setting surface for tile.

Forms Structures usually made of 2×6s or other framing lumber to contain concrete as it cures.

Glaze A hard surface generally fired onto the exposed side of a ceramic tile, which imparts a glossy shine.

Greenboard A water-resistant variety of drywall used in kitchens and bathrooms.

Grout A slurry troweled into joints between tiles that fills the seams and solidifies the tile field. Available in many formulas and colors.

Grout float A rubber-surfaced trowel used to apply grout to tiled surfaces.

Grout sealer Typically a clear coating such as silicone used to protect porous grout and facilitate cleaning.

Layout stick A straight, long, narrow board marked in increments of tile widths and grout joints.

Lugs Small projections, also called nubs, formed into tile edges to maintain even spacing.

Mastic Common term for organic-based adhesives.

Mortar The mixture of sand, cement, and water used to float beds for tile.

Metal lath Light-gauge metal reinforcing sheets often used to strengthen mortar beds (thickset) under tile.

Mosaic Small tiles that are used to create a design or pattern, generally sold in preassembled sheets.

Mud Tile-setter's term for mortar applied in a setting bed.

Nonvitreous tile A porous tile that absorbs moisture and is not resistant to freeze-thaw cycles.

Notched trowel A metal trowel with notches along one or more sides used to rake out ribs of adhesive to a specified height.

Open time The length of time adhesive can stay on a surface before it dries out, skins over, and no longer forms an effective bond.

Organic mastic A premixed oil- or water-based tile adhesive generally with less bond strength and water resistance than other thinsets.

Pot life The maximum time that a mixed adhesive will stay flexible enough to spread and create a good bond.

Running bond A basic tile pattern that alters the standard grid alignment, with tiles on one course staggered one-half the tile width from the tiles in the course below.

Score To scratch or etch a cut line in a tile or other material so that it will break in a clean line.

Sheet-mounted tile Any small-size tile mounted with spaced grout seams to a sheet or mesh backer for easier application.

Shower-floor membrane A flexible waterproof material under tile that protects against leak damage by directing any water that seeps through seams into the weep holes of the shower drain.

Snap cutter A hand-powered tile cutter with a scoring head that travels on metal guides and a raised rib over which the tile is snapped.

Squeegee A flexible, rubber-edge tool used to clean excess grout off of a tiled surface.

Subfloor Plywood panels (or tongue-and-groove boards in older homes) installed over joists to support finished flooring material.

Substrate The supporting layer under tile, generally panels of plywood or backer board.

Thickset The term used for tile installations that use a thick bed of mortar between tile and substrate. Generally used on older installations, while thin beds of adhesive are generally used today.

Thinset The term for modern tile installations that use a thin ribbed coat of adhesive between the tile and substrate.

Thinset mortar The term generally used to describe any of the cement-based tile adhesives.

Tile nippers Similar to a pair of pliers, with strong biting blades used to break away small bits of tile to create cuts that are not in a straight line.

Tile spacers Cross-shaped pieces of plastic, available in many sizes, placed at the corners of newly laid tiles to maintain even spacing throughout a layout.

Underlayment Smooth panels of plywood or backer board used as a base for setting tile.

V-cap tile A basically L-shaped tile with a slightly raised corner commonly used along the edges of kitchen and bath countertops.

Vitreous tile A dense, strong, nonporous tile that is resistant to freeze-thaw cycles.

Wet saw A power tool with a circular, diamond-edged blade that trims individual tiles. The blade is lubricated by a stream of water that is collected in a pan beneath the tile and recirculated.

Waterproof membrane A flexible rubberlike material used in tiled tub and shower installations, and also in thickset counter installations.

Zero clearance Term that applies to prefab fireplace units that can be installed next to framing and other combustible materials.

Index

Index

Index

Index

Metric Equivalents

Length

1 inch	25.4mm
1 foot	0.3048m
1 yard	0.9144m
1 mile	1.61km

Area

1 square inch	645mm^2
1 square foot	0.0929m^2
1 square yard	0.8361m^2
1 acre	4046.86m^2
1 square mile	2.59km^2

Volume

1 cubic inch	16.3870cm^3
1 cubic foot	0.03m^3
1 cubic yard	0.77m^3

Common Lumber Equivalents

Sizes: Metric cross sections are so close to their U.S. sizes, as noted below, that for most purposes they may be considered equivalents.

Dimensional lumber	1 x 2	19 x 38mm
	1 x 4	19 x 89mm
	2 x 2	38 x 38mm
	2 x 4	38 x 89mm
	2 x 6	38 x 140mm
	2 x 8	38 x 184mm
	2 x 10	38 x 235mm
	2 x 12	38 x 286mm
Sheet sizes	4 x 8 ft.	1200 x 2400mm
	4 x 10 ft.	1200 x 3000mm
Sheet thicknesses	¼ in.	6mm
	⅜ in.	9mm
	½ in.	12mm
	¾ in.	19mm
Stud/joist spacing	16 in. o.c.	400mm o.c.
	24 in. o.c.	600mm o.c.

Capacity

1 fluid ounce	29.57mL
1 pint	473.18mL
1 quart	0.95L
1 gallon	3.79L

Weight

1 ounce	28.35g
1 pound	0.45kg

Temperature

Fahrenheit = Celsius x 1.8 + 32
Celsius = Fahrenheit - 32 x ⁵/₉

Nail Size and Length

Penny Size	Nail Length
2d	1"
3d	1¼"
4d	1½"
5d	1¾"
6d	2"
7d	2¼"
8d	2½"
9d	2¾"
10d	3"
12d	3¼"
16d	3½"

Photo Credits

All photography by John Parsekian/CH, unless otherwise noted.

Front cover: *main* Henry Willson; *left top* Mark Lohman; *left center* Phillip H. Ennis Photography, architect: Elizabeth Steimberg; *left bottom:* davidduncanlivingston.com **Page 1:** Mark Lohman **page 2:** Tony Giammarino/Giammarino & Dworkin **page 5:** *bottom* Neal Barrett/CH **page 7:** Tony Giammarino/Giammarino & Dworkin **page 8:** Mark Lohman **page 9:** Mark Lohman **page 10:** Mark Lohman **page 11:** center Mark Samu, architect: Bruce Nagle, AIA **page 12–13:** *top* JC Carton/Carto/Bruce Coleman, Inc.; *bottom right* ME Jordan/Bruce Coleman, Inc.; *bottom left* Phillip H. Ennis Photography **page 14:** Susan Teare, builder: Reap Construction, LTD **page 15:** *top* Brian Vanden Brink; center *both* courtesy of Abbate Tile; *bottom both* David Phelps **page 18:** *left* Mark Lohman; *right* Jessie Walker, architect: Lenore Weiss Baigelman, Full Circle Architects **page 19:** *top left* Mark Samu, architect: Bruce Nagle, AIA; *top right* & *bottom* Jessie Walker **page 20:** Phillip H. Ennis Photography, design: Anne Cooper Interiors **page 21:** *top left* Anne Gummerson; *bottom left* Phillip H. Ennis Photography, design: Amir Ilin, Kuche Cuchina; *bottom right* Mark Samu, architect: Andy Levtovsky, AIA; *top right* davidduncanlivingston.com **page 22:** Brian Vanden Brink **page 23:** *top left* Brian Vanden Brink; *top right* Stickley Photo•Graphic; *bottom right* Mark Samu, design: Lucianna Samu Design; *bottom left* Phillip H. Ennis Photography **page 24:** Stickley Photo•Graphic **page 25:** *top right* Mark Samu, stylist: Tia Burns; *top left* Jessie Walker, design: Dave Hagerman; *bottom* Phillip H. Ennis Photograaphy, design: Diane Lowenthal, Lowenthal & Partners **page 26:** *left* Mark Lohman; *right* Tony Giammarino/Giammarino & Dworkin **page 27:** *top* Phillip H. Ennis Photography, architect: Opacic Architects; *bottom left* Brian Vanden Brink; *bottom right* Jessie Walker, design: Dave McFadden, Past Basket Cabinetry **page 28:** Stickley Photo•Graphic, design: Pratt & Larson Tile & Stone **page 29:** *top left* Mark Lohman; *top right* Phillip H. Ennis Photography, design: Salem Hill Studios; *bottom right* Tony Giammarino/Giammarino & Dworkin, builder: Sue Kipp Construction; *bottom left* Tony Giammarino/Giammarino & Dworkin, design Marge Thomas **pages 30–31:** *all* Mark Lohman

page 32: *left* Phillip H. Ennis Photography; *right* Mark Samu/courtesy of Hearst Magazines **page 33:** *top left* Phillip H. Ennis Photography; *top right* Eric Roth; *bottom* Phillip H. Ennis Photography, design: Stephanie Wolf, M&S Associates **page 56:** Tony Giammarino/Giammarino & Dworkin **page 58:** *both* courtesy of Abbate Tile **page 59:** Susan Teare, architect/builder: Studio III Architects and Silver Maple Construction **page 60:** courtesy of American Olean **page 61:** *left* courtesy of Abbate; *right* Phillip H. Ennis Photography **page 66:** Jerry Pavia **pages 78–81:** *all* Neal Barrett **page 82:** *top left* Jessie Walker, architect: Lenore Baigelman, Full Circle Architects; *top right* & *bottom right* Tony Giammarino/Giammarino & Dworkin; *top left* Mark Samu/courtesy of Hearst Magaines **page 83:** Stickley Photo•Graphic **page 84:** *bottom left* Mark Samu; *top right* melabee m miller, design: Camille Waldron; *bottom right* melabee m miller, design: Mock Fox Interiors **page 85:** Brian Vanden Brink **page 86:** Mark Lohman **page 87:** center Merle Henkenius **page 88:** courtesy of Maticad **page 89:** *top* courtesy of DalTile; *bottom both* courtesy of Maticad **pages 94–97:** *all* Merle Henkenius **page 104:** *bottom left* and *top* Mark Lohman; *bottom right* Tony Giammarino/Giammarino & Dworkin **page 105:** Tony Giammarino/Giammarino & Dworkin **page 106:** *top left* Stickley Photo•Graphic; *top right* Mark Lohman; *bottom* Peter Tata, design: James Carroll **page 107:** *top* Jessie Walker, design: Arlene Semel; *bottom right* Mark Lohman; *bottom left* Tony Giammarino/Giammarino & Dworkin **page 108:** *both* Stickley Photo•Graphic **page 109:** *top left* davidduncanlivingston.com; *right* Phillip H. Ennis Photography, architect: Elizabeth Steimberg; *bottom left* Tria Giovan **page 110:** Mark Lohman **page 112:** Tony Giammarino/Giammarino & Dworkin **page 116:** *bottom* Jerry Pavia **page 128–131:** *all* Steve Willson **pages 132–133:** *all* Neal Barrett/CH **page 134:** Tony Giammarino/Giammarino & Dworkin **page 135:** *bottom left* and *top left* Mark Lohman; *right* Tony Giammarino/Giammarino & Dworkin **page 136:** *top right* Mark Samu, design: Sherrill Canet Design; *bottom* Mark Lohman; *top left* Tony Giammarino/Giammarino & Dworkin **page 137:** Mark Lohman **page 138:** *top right* Mark Lohman; *bottom right* Tony Giammarino/Giammarino & Dworkin; *left* Ivy Moriber-Neal/Ivy D Photography **page 139:** Stickley

Photo•Graphic, design: O'Leal & Associates **page 140:** Mark Lohman **page 145:** Tony Giammarino/Giammarino & Dworkin **page 150:** Tria Giovan **page 152:** Susan Teare, architect/builder: Elizabeth Herrmann Architecture + Design and Northern Timbers Construction **page 160:** *left* and *top right* Mark Lohman; *bottom right* Jerry Pavia **page 161:** *top* Mark Lohman; *bottom* Susan Teare, architect: Brad Rabinowitz Architect **page 162:** melabee m miller, design Deck House, LLC **page 163:** *top left* Mark Samu, design: Kitchens by Ken Kelly; *top right* Mark Samu, design: Durst Construction; *bottom right* Roger Turk, design: Showplace Design & Remodeling; *bottom left* Brian Vanden Brink **page 164:** *top right* courtesy of Artistic Tile, Geometrica; *bottom right* courtesy of Artistic Tile, Hamptons Blend; *bottom left* Tony Giammarino/Giammarino & Dworkin **page 166:** Mark Lohman **page 168:** *bottom* Jerry Pavia **page 174:** K. Rice/H. Armstrong Roberts **page 176:** Grey Crawford **page 178:** Stickley Photo•Graphic **page 179:** *left* Mark Lohman; *top right* Mark Samu, builder: Access Builders; *bottom right* Tony Giammarino/Giammarino & Dworkin **page 180:** *top left* melabee m miller, design: Karen Shapiro; *right* Stickley Photo•Graphic; *bottom left* Tony Giammarino/Giammarino & Dworkin **page 181:** Stickley Photo•Graphic, design: Pratt & Larson Tile & Stone **page 182:** *left* Mark Lohman; *top right* Jerry Pavia; *bottom right* Jerry Pavia **page 183:** Mark Lohman **page 184:** Mark Lohman **page 186:** *bottom* Jessie Walker **page 189:** *top left* courtesy of American Olean; *top right* Crandall & Crandall **page 195:** courtesy of Inma Roca Associates **page 196:** *top right* & *top left* Stickley Photo•Graphic; *bottom right* Mark Lohman; *bottom right* Jerry Pavia, design: Irina & Erik Gronborg **page 197:** Mark Lohman **page 198:** Mark Lohman **page 199:** *top* Jerry Pavia; *right* Tony Giammarino/Giammarino & Dworkin; *bottom* and *left* Mark Lohman **pages 200–201:** *all* Brian Vanden Brink **page 202:** Mark Lohman **page 206:** *top right* courtesy of American Olean **page 214:** Mark Lohman **page 216:** Jerry Pavia **page 218:** Mark Lohman **page 220:** Bradley Olman **page 222:** Roger Turk **page 226:** Tony Giammarino/Giammarino & Dworkin **page 227:** Mark Lohman **page 228:** Jerry Pavia **page 233:** Mark Lohman **page 236:** Tria Giovan

Have a home improvement or gardening project?
Look for these and other fine Creative Homeowner books
wherever books are sold

EASY CLOSETS
Introduces homeowners to the variety of closet types and closet systems available.

Over 275 photographs.
160 pp.
8½" x 10⅞"
$14.95 (US)
BOOK #: CH277135

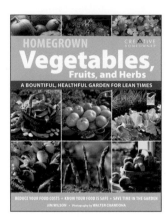

HOMEGROWN VEGETABLES
A complete guide to growing your own vegetables, fruits, and herbs.

Over 275 photographs and illustrations.
192 pp.
8½" x 10⅞"
$16.95 (US)
BOOK #: CH274551

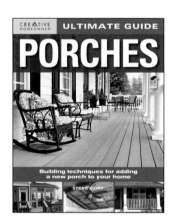

ULTIMATE GUIDE PORCHES
Step-by-Step guide to design and build a porch.

Over 300 photographs.
192 pp.
8½" x 10⅞"
$16.95 (US)
BOOK #: CH277970

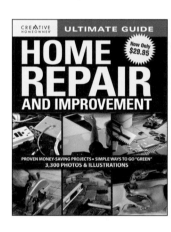

ULTIMATE GUIDE: HOME REPAIR, 3rd Ed.
The ultimate home-improvement reference manual.

Over 3,300 photos and illustrations. 608 pp.;
9¼" x 10⅞"
$29.95 (US)
BOOK #: CH267880

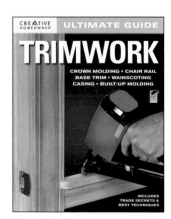

ULTIMATE GUIDE: TRIMWORK
Transform a room with trimwork.

Over 975 photos and illustrations.
288 pp.;
8½" x 10⅞"
$19.95 (US)
BOOK #: CH277511

ULTIMATE GUIDE: WIRING, 7th Ed.
Explains residential electrical systems in easy-to-understand terms.

Over 950 full-color photos and illustrations.
304 pages
8½" x 10⅞"
$18.95 (US)
BOOK #: CH278240

For more information and to order direct, go to **www.creativehomeowner.com**